Ancient Peoples and Places

JAPAN

General Editor

DR GLYN DANIEL

Bridle-bit from Ōtani tomb

Ancient Peoples and Places

JAPAN

BEFORE BUDDHISM

J. E. Kidder Jr

108 PHOTOGRAPHS
65 LINE DRAWINGS
AND 7 MAPS

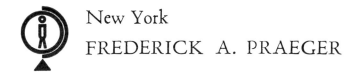

New York
FREDERICK A. PRAEGER

THIS IS VOLUME TEN IN THE SERIES

Ancient Peoples and Places

GENERAL EDITOR: DR GLYN DANIEL

BOOKS THAT MATTER   *Published in the United States of America in 1959 by Frederick A. Praeger, Inc., Publishers, 15 West 47th Street, New York 36, N.Y.*
All rights reserved
Library of Congress Catalog Card Number: 59-7038
Printed in Great Britain

CONTENTS

CONTENTS

6

ILLUSTRATIONS

14

Alfred Salmony. In Memoriam

Acknowledgements

I T WOULD NOT HAVE BEEN POSSIBLE to complete this book if Japanese archaeologists had not been so generous with their aid and counsel. I am particularly grateful to a number who kindly supplied me with the needed photographs. These include Dr Kyoichi Arimitsu and Professor Takayasu Higuchi of Kyōto University who provided me with a wide selection, the latter allowing me to use unpublished illustrations; Mr Yukio Kobayashi of the same institute, who permitted me to reproduce a photograph; Dr Jirō Harada and Mr Kyosuke Yajima, who furnished me with the photographs and gave me permission to illustrate objects in the National Museum, Tokyo; Dr Masao Suenaga who generously allowed me to reproduce certain illustrations from one of his books; Mr Sugao Yamanouchi who permitted me to illustrate vessels in the Department of Anthropology, Tokyo University; and similarly to Mr Eishi Nishihara of the Bureau of Archives and Mausolea, Imperial Palace; Mr Yoshio Yamasaki; and to Mr Teizo Tani I am indebted for permission to use photographs.

On a more local level, my assistant, Mrs Sanae Kawamura, rendered long, arduous and indispensable services; with an unerring eye, Mr Takashi Sōma, my durable travelling companion, was able to locate sites in an expeditious way. My wife has used a lightly guiding hand in trying to maintain the right perspective and eliminating abstruse spots in the writing, but she need hardly be blamed for any mysteries that may remain. To these and others I would like to express my sincere appreciation, for they all have given liberally of their time and effort.

While the manuscript was in production, my long-time professor at New York University, Dr Alfred Salmony, died on the way to Europe. With more extensive documentation even he might have approved of this book. To the memory of a genuine friend, this volume is respectfully dedicated.

J.E.K.

Introduction

THE FOUR MAIN ISLANDS and the many hundreds of smaller ones that make up the country of Japan are stretched along a slender arc that resembles a façade for the North Asian continent. Most of these islands lie within a temperate zone, and an inventory of those that have at one time or another been dominated by Japan would include the southern Kuriles, Sakhalin below the 50° parallel, and at the other end of the chain, the Ryūkyū Islands and Formosa. These extremities of course came under the influence of the Honshū government in recent times, yet this is the area which has much homogeneity in early prehistoric periods. The Stone Age under consideration extended over 1,500 miles—from a point north of Hokkaidō to Okinawa—but in the period corresponding with the use of bronze, a metal-influenced culture, though not necessarily bronze itself, penetrated beyond Kyūshū, but not as far as Okinawa, and into the southern Tōhoku district of North Honshū. Later, under the proto-historic rulers in the Yamato Plain the tightening of political controls brought a further shrinking of the lines and the establishment of a sphere of sovereignty that was to remain virtually unchanged for centuries. During the long centuries of history that these borders were maintained, the distinctions between races became increasingly sharpened and the dividing lines between cultures more clearly delineated. This area of protohistoric and historic Japan encompasses the islands of Kyūshū, Shikoku and that part of Honshū that lies below the 39° parallel.

Various names are given to the different regions of Japan, and it seems preferable to use those that are in current use and most understood by westerners, although in so doing one draws criticism from certain archaeological circles. North Honshū has been traditionally referred to as Tōhoku (the north-east); the west side, Hokuriku (region of the north country). The Kantō Plain, to a great extent the hinterland of Tokyo, includes the prefectures of Chiba, Ibaragi, Saitama, Kanagawa, and the lower regions of Tochigi and Gumma, as well as a slice of Yamanashi. It takes an irregular shape with long fingers of lowland that reach into the mountains. The Tōsan (east mountains) is the mountainous part of central Honshū, while the Chūbu (middle region) overlaps it to some extent, but runs almost exactly north and south. From Nagano prefecture to the south coast around Shizuoka, the name Shinshū is frequently used. The Tōkaidō (region of the eastern sea) through which the famous road from Kyōto to Tokyo runs and from which the road received its name, is chiefly the coastal strip that connects the Yamato and Kantō Plains. Much of this band is mountainous, and its division into fifty-three units, famed as posting-stations in the Edo period, gives a picture of how long the journey took before the introduction of twentieth-century modes of transportation. Since the Kantō includes the northern part of this Tōkai region, the Tōkai term is most useful for that area which swings down through Shizuoka and Aichi past the Ise Bay to join with the Kansai. The Kyōto-Ōsaka district goes by a number of names depending on which time-period one is referring to, or how broad a context is intended. Historically it is the Gō-Kinai (five provinces): Yamashiro, Yamato, Kawachi, Settsu and Izumi; geographically it is the Kansai, the western end of the mountains of which Kantō stands at the east. Another name, Kinki, is sometimes used in a more inclusive sense, and by most lines of reasoning may be employed to incorporate its southern extension, the Kii Peninsula. Farther to the south and making up the lower third of Honshū is Chūgoku (middle provinces). On the outer side lies the

Sanindō (land in mountain shade); on the Inland Sea side, the Sanyōdō (land exposed to the mountains). The islands of Shikoku (four provinces) and Kyūshū (nine provinces) received their names by common consent from already established subdivisions.

Archaeological work was started in Japan on a serious scale when the country was still organized into about sixty-six provinces (*kuni*), although the number varies with the date under consideration. The Meiji Restoration instituted the prefectural system, but many adjustments were necessary before it was fully enforced and today's forty-six prefectures materialized. The finds, files and catalogues for half a century were all recorded in terms of the old provinces. The change has been painful; the provinces have died hard; and to add to the archaeologists' problems of transposition, the dividing lines of the old provinces and the new prefectures are often not the same. The current method of streamlining and redistributing administered land requires constant revision of files as place-names are swallowed up by expanding cities, towns or villages. In view of the fact that an enlightened estimate would judge there to be in the neighbourhood of 100,000 sites (three-fourths Neolithic), which are generously distributed over usable land far less than the area of 142,000 square miles that makes up the four islands of Japan, archaeologists have been forced to devise an adequate way of distinguishing one from the other, particularly since they may frequently lie only a few hundred yards apart. Sites are therefore invariably recorded by prefecture (*ken*), county (*gun*), village (*mura*), and a number of other qualifying words that may indicate the vicinity (*Aza, Ōaza,* etc.). When applicable, city (*shi*) replaces the county, and within it is the ward (*ku*), and a more pinpointed address. All this is essential for the pursuit of archaeological studies in Japan, but for a book of this nature and to the western reader lacking detailed maps in Japanese, it is not very useful.

It goes without saying that the discovery of so many sites and the recording of even a small percentage of them means there has been intense archaeological work and accompanying publication for many decades, accelerating in recent years. A newly published (1958) and complete bibliography of the Stone Age up to 1955 lists 3,869 references. Many of the larger sites, such as the shell-mounds that cover up to 40,000 or more square feet, have been dug and redug until they are worn out and, like the Ōmori mounds, may not have a shell left. They have thus become the subject for a steady stream of reports.

The story is often told how modern archaeology began in Japan when Professor Edward S. Morse arrived and noticed that the shell debris was an indication of Neolithic habitation on the islands. In this dramatic way Morse set to work in 1879 to excavate the mounds at Ōmori on the railway line between Yokohama and Tokyo. His publication in English, *Shell Mounds of Omori*, started the long procession of site reports that increases by the year. As more remains were discovered, ideas concerning this culture slowly began to take shape. Shōgoro Tsuboi held the first chair of anthropology at Tokyo University, and another leading figure, Ryūzō Torii, spanned the fields of anthropology and ethnology in prehistoric and Ainu studies. In 1929 Kashiwa Ōyama founded the Institute of Prehistory, and concentrated on Neolithic excavations for fifteen years until the centre was wiped out during the war. Many of the gilt-edged names in archaeology made their reputations in this academic atmosphere and on the pages of its publications, the *Shizengaku Zasshi* (or *Zeitschrift für Praehistorie*, as he titled it in German). A real understanding of chronology in the Stone Age based on pottery typology was evolving and perspective was given in 1937 by Sugao Yamanouchi when he set up five divisions within which were fixed successive types. Neolithic passions have run toward filling out chronologies with pottery types since that time. This period became familiarly known as the *Jōmon* period, after the com⁄mon use of cord⁄marking for decorating the pottery. It is particularly strong in North Honshū, in the Kantō Plain where almost a thousand shell⁄mounds have been discovered, and in the central mountains. Perhaps because it was super⁄seded earlier in South Japan by the Bronze⁄Iron Age, it appears there as a thinner layer, overshadowed in importance by the metal periods.

In 1884 at Yayoi⁄machi in the Hongō section of Tokyo another major pottery type was discovered. Of a wheel⁄made nature and largely undecorated, it turned out to be associated with objects that corresponded to the Bronze Age, and pro⁄vided the impetus needed to see the initiation of studies that were eventually to clarify the characteristics of this period. Traditionally this is the *Yayoi* period. Actual and often very extensive digging has been necessary to uncover information on this age: villages, remains of paddy fields, cemeteries and small hoards have come to light, and fortunately many of these discoveries were not made until excavations had taken on a more scientific nature in the nineteen⁄thirties and later. The talents of Japanese scientists to work together as a team have been particularly effective in large⁄scale research on these sites, and universities and the government⁄sponsored Commission for the Protection of Cultural Properties have published informative results.

In some ways research on the Iron Age or protohistoric period was slower to materialize, perhaps partly because of the sacred character of the literature that records the events at the early imperial court during these centuries and the lack of any need or desire to inquire into it. Kōsaku Hamada of Kyōto University, in utilizing comparative Far Eastern materials, brought archaeological work out of the insularity of local studies and into the light of international recognition by 1920. These years witnessed the first systematic investigations of hundreds of tumuli that are the visible remains of the early aristocratic class, in work that was carried on by the Kyōto group under the direction of Sueji Umehara. Four decades of energetic research by Umehara resulted in his authorship of a hundred books and nine times as many articles on Far Eastern archaeology. Prefectural governments also sponsored surveys and excavations of tombs and other sites within their juris-diction. Now all the major universities have well-staffed archaeology departments which constantly conduct regular excavations and frequent emergency salvage operations. Government safeguarding of sites and their preservation has been an important factor that archaeologists have welcomed, although vandalism is still a major problem. Post-war develop-ments in new construction work of all sorts have made the shielding and rescue of important sites a pressing question, as it is in many other countries.

Mountains are the most prominent geographical feature of Japan, three systems creating main divisions in the country. The Sakhalin chain runs through Hokkaidō, down Honshū like a spine, and forms the high central mountains in the Nagano area, coming out around Shizuoka, east of Nagoya. Another chain crosses Kyūshū and Shikoku, runs somewhat south of Ōsaka and Kyōto and more or less meets the Sakhalin chain in the Nagano and Shizuoka region. Lying about at right angles to these, and virtually bisecting Japan, is the Fuji Group. The Izu and Noto Peninsulas on the east and west mark the approximate line of these mountains, popularly referred to as the Japan Alps. It goes without saying that many chains still contain active volcanoes.

Ammonite and other fossils indicate that some if not most sections of Japan were under water during the Palaeozoic era, a period in which rather violent volcanic activity must have taken place. Towards the end of the Palaeozoic the elevation of the land began to expose large areas above water, and mountain ranges started to take shape. Although rising and lowering never ceased, during the Mesozoic Japan must have been joined with the continent through Korea, Manchuria and southern Russia. There is some indication that it may at one time have been connected in a southerly direction with the Philippine Islands and Java. In the Miocene and Pliocene of the Cenozoic the land began to sink again, probably in two major shifts. Accidental discoveries of animal fossils, chiefly of the elephant and deer families, show that the land formation was considerably different from that of the present day. Large areas of central and North-west Hokkaidō, the west side of Honshū, and the east-coast peninsulas were more than likely not visible. During the Pleistocene these sections filled them-selves out, and the same process is still at work today. Should this trend persist, the vast hunting-grounds of the early mam-mals may once again be exposed. Elephant fossils, for instance, have been pulled from the bed of the Inland Sea by fishermen, and remains of these animals have now been discovered in the scattered regions of Aomori, Tochigi, Tokyo, Gifu, Waka-yama and Hyōgo. Pliocene and later fauna include the following members of the elephant family: *Stegodon orientalis*, *Stegodon sinensis*, *Parelephas protomammonteus*, *Elephas trogontheri*, *Elephas namadicus*, *Elephas indicus*, and in addition the giraffe, all known on the continent. The arctic hairy mammoth (*Elephas primigenius*) crossed from Siberia in the latter part of the Pliocene, and his fossils have been found in Sakhalin and Hokkaidō, but not yet on Honshū. It was probably too warm for him on the more southerly islands. If a warm climate accompanied the elephant, the likelihood of much rainfall would have accounted for heavy forestation, and would have forced early man to the edges of wooded areas and sea coasts as the most habitable regions. If Palaeolithic man lived in Japan in any appreciable numbers, the bulk of his remains are probably under the present sea-level. To have lived on these islands, his trek must have begun at a time when he could cross by land; whereas Neolithic man, on the other hand, in his dugout canoe would never have been for long out of sight of land, whether he came up from southern islands, crossed from Korea, or entered from the continent via Sakhalin and Hokkaidō.

CHAPTER I

The Palaeolithic and Mesolithic Periods

THE DISCOVERY IN 1949 at Iwajuku, Gumma, of stone implements in a stratum believed to be lower than that in which Kantō Plain pottery is usually found marked the beginning of the current pursuit of the Palaeolithic culture in Japan. Before that date there had been strong proponents of an Old Stone Age, but the scattered and often unconvincing objects, and what seemed to be exaggerated claims, may have actually delayed full cognizance of their significance.

Geologists and archaeologists alike do not all concur with the Palaeolithic designation, and the terms 'non-pottery' or 'pre-pottery', used by many, seem to have had general acceptance. Geologists might prefer to find more definite proof that these remains actually belong to the Pleistocene or to see them in a fossil animal context, but in both a technological and economic sense the pre-pottery discoveries appear to qualify as Palaeolithic. But also by these criteria, at least the earliest phase of the Jōmon period belongs to the Mesolithic. Sites of the Jōmon period are so frequently characterized by a profusion of pottery fragments that when pottery is not found together with stone implements an immediate and proper question of relationships arises. The stone implements themselves cannot provide the entire answer simply because the break is not complete between the pre-Jōmon and early Jōmon types, therefore the geological circumstances of the discovery play an important role. Moreover, while the temptation to call any site containing Palaeolith-like implements anterior to Jōmon times is obviously great, a glance at the last compilation of the Stone Age sites in Japan—a work of 1928 and not continued because the cataloguing of such rapid discoveries obviously became hopeless—

will show only stone objects from quite a few hundred of the approximately ten thousand sites there listed (*List of Stone Age Sites in Japan*, Tokyo University, fifth edition, 1928).

The question of date in the Kantō region is undoubtedly associated with the formation of the upper layers of the Plain. Humus of a few inches to two or more feet lies over the Kantō loam; the loam was laid down in a series of layers as volcanic ash, wind deposited, and varies in depth to approximately six feet in places. The variation in thickness is probably chiefly due to the distance from the source: Mt Fuji would have been responsible for most of the deposits in the south-western part of the Plain, Mts Asama, Akagi and Haruna for those in the west. Until recently it was believed that Japan was already a group of islands when the loam was formed. Jōmon period remains are almost always found in the thin topmost layer of soil, and when certain pottery types do occur in the Kantō loam, they are logically recognized as the earliest. This of course means also that archaeological remains will never be at great depth, and frequently excavation reveals little more than one can gather right on the surface.

After the discovery of stone implements at Iwajuku well down in the loam layer, geologists took another look at the problem of the Kantō loam. It had been considered to be Late Pleistocene in formation; perhaps it belongs rather to the Middle Pleistocene, or in other words before the islands detached themselves from the continent. At least to consider it so would obviously leave the way open for the makers of Iwajuku period stone tools to reach Honshū by land.

Two layers of the loam at Iwajuku contained stone pieces. The Iwajuku dark brown clay bed, the lower of the two, extends to an average depth of six feet below the surface. In this

Fig. 1a

layer two hand-axe core tools with retouched edges, labelled Iwajuku I, were found. They are sometimes referred to as flake tools in this case, and along with two scrapers and a few blade flakes, are mostly of shale. Iwajuku II, the lower part of the Azami yellow-brown sand layer, directly above, consisted of small end- and side-scrapers, as well as discarded flakes, chips and cores. Light blue agate is the material of the majority; many are of obsidian, some of shale and andesite. Iwajuku III remains a question-mark, partly because before careful work

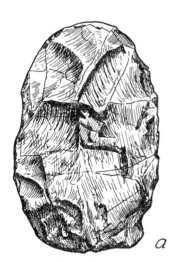  

Fig. 1   Stone implements of pre-pottery periods: (a) Iwajuku, Gumma, $3\frac{3}{4}''$, (b) Takei, Gumma, (c) Sanwa, Hokkaidō, $7\frac{3}{8}''$

could be undertaken a number of stone pieces were removed, but there is some suggestion that small tools of a scraper type, microlithic in form, may have made up this stage. Inaridai pottery, one of the earliest Jōmon types, was discovered on a hillside in the vicinity in a layer that seemed to be nearer the surface than these stone tools.

Now that numerous sites have been tagged 'pre-pottery', one would expect to see certain patterns unfolding. There is a profusion of types and consistency is elusive, but core tools and retouched flakes as general categories make up the lion's share of the artifacts. Japanese archaeologists speak in terms of three major tool types: the hand-axe, points, and blades. Hand-axe sites are known along the Inland Sea, on the western side of the Kantō Plain, and in the southern, eastern and northern parts of Hokkaidō. Points are more profuse in the Inland Sea region and in the central mountains. They were first found in the Tōhoku in 1957 at Amako in Yamagata, and have never been plentiful in Hokkaidō. The blades are largely northern in distribution, concentrated mainly in Hok-kaidō in over ten sites, though also found in the southern Tōhoku and Tōsan. One Inland Sea site has yielded them.

Fig. 1b

At Takei (Niisato), Gumma, and Moro (Itabashi ward), Tokyo, sharply pointed blades of obsidian are worked on one face only. The Chausuyama implements, also of obsidian, are blades or scrapers produced from flakes, retouched on one side in most cases; and not far away, at Uenodaira in Suwa City, Nagano, laurel-leaf-shaped points, along with flakes and chips, are in the same readily accessible volcanic stone. Flakes are rather popular through the central mountains; Yabuzuka is not far from Iwajuku, and at Yadegawa (Maki), Nagano, cores and fine slender flakes were located.

While many of these reported stone implement finds are from the surface, greater reliability is attached to those that are the result of systematic digging. Tarukishi in the neighbour-hood of Hakodate city, South Hokkaidō, yielded large blades, side- and end-scrapers, a core and flakes at a depth of approxi-mately a foot and a half. The neat shale blades in some cases exceed six inches in length.

Fig. 10

Concerning himself with typological similarities on a wider horizon, Maringer, after examining tools from Gongenyama near Isezaki city, Gumma, finds the early and middle cultural layers at that site to have contained implements that have affinities with the Lower Palaeolithic Patjitanian industry of Java. The chopping tools, the flakes that have a pseudo-Levalloisian look, and blades together with a blade-core, all show some similarities to Javan types.[1]

Out of this *mélange* Sugihara proposes with caution succes-sive stages based on geological stratigraphy as follows:[2] (using the loose Japanese term *bunka* as culture).

Geological strata	Chief types	Cultural site-term
	Mature point culture	Uenodaira culture
	Early stages of point culture	Takei II culture
Yellowish-brown clay layer of Kantō loam	Mature blade culture	Chausuyama culture
	Multi-type blade culture	Moro culture
	Pointed knife culture	Iwajuku II culture
Dark brown clay layer of Kantō loam	Early stages of blade culture	Takei I culture
	Hand-axe culture	Iwajuku I culture

There is still considerable question as to whether the points actually precede the appearance of pottery. The Motonoki site in Niigata provided the controversy that has forced more intensive efforts to determine the relative position of the points. The geological layers are not easily separated, and the issue hinges on whether the nearby pottery belongs to a layer higher than the points or to the same stratum. This problem will eventually resolve itself with greater satisfaction when more sites are discovered in which pottery is directly associated in vertical stratigraphy with the stone industry, but as Japanese sites are shallow and earth movements have been frequent, one can hardly place full confidence in these implied relationships. As an argument on either side of the question, one may point to innumerable instances in Jōmon period sites in which many thousands of years of pottery types are thoroughly mixed. Perhaps the most striking is the Kyūgo cave in Gifu that was excavated by Nagoya University. Ten pottery classes ranging from the earliest to the latest and therefore spanning a minimum of four millennia were taken out of a layer averaging two feet in thickness in which no significant stratigraphy in types was discernible. Both Jōmon and Yayoi man occupied the cave, and some of the retouched flake tools which came to light may be taken to indicate either that pre-pottery man used the cave as a shelter, or that here was a case of co-existence of pottery and certain of the so-called non-pottery implement types.

While agreement is not unanimous on terminology, there is much to support the use of the term 'Mesolithic' for the microlithic industries and early pottery stages. There is un-questionably some overlap in time, and the two are here linked inasmuch as pottery and microliths are found together in certain early Jōmon sites, notably Tado in Yokosuka city. But the Jōmon period does not readily provide lines of distinc-tion between the Mesolithic and Neolithic, although the assumption has generally been that the terms 'Jōmon' and 'Neolithic' are synonymous. There can be no doubt that the two terms become more and more conflated as time passes.

The Iijima excavation of Kagawa Prefecture, an Inland Sea island that actually lies opposite Tamano city, Okayama, represents a fertile industry that includes very small flake blades, sometimes less than a half-inch in length; retouched bifaced points; and cores. It need not all be specifically pre-pottery because of the number of projectile points that hardly seem to differ from those of the Jōmon period; there is variety in the shape of these points, but chiefly they are nearly triangular with concave base.

The Jōmon period may be characterized throughout most of its evolution as a retarded Neolithic, and even over-run in south Japan by the Bronze and Iron Ages before country-wide maturity had been attained. Only primitive agriculture on a small scale seems to have been known, domestication of animals is not definitely established before the last millennium of the development, and small community life near heaps of shell debris or along river banks must have been organized with a view towards greater effectiveness in gathering and hunting as well as for mutual protection, but not as farming communities in the developed sense.

CHAPTER II

The Neolithic Period

THE MAJOR SUBDIVISIONS within the Jōmon period have been built around families of pottery types which Yamanouchi visualized as forming five stages in the evolution.[3] These divisions are broad enough not to require a specific knowledge of the pottery typology and handy when the type cannot be easily ascertained, yet are sufficiently narrow to fix the material under consideration within a time span of about a thousand years, which for Jōmon dating is often not too imprecise. The Japanese names of these periods, *Sō-ki*, *Zen-ki*, *Chū-ki*, *Ko-ki* and *Ban-ki*, can hardly all be literally translated into the less picturesque English, but their equivalents may be Earliest, Early, Middle, Late and Latest; or, as Groot used them, Proto-Jōmon, Early-, Middle-, Later- and Final-Jōmon.[4] The value of such divisions is fully recognized, but they are primarily applicable to Honshū, and some archaeologists working in Kyūshū and Hokkaidō maintain separate methods: Early, Middle and Late for Kyūshū; and after the early stages in Hokkaidō, a Zenhoku (Early Northern), and Kohoku (Late Northern), along with site-types, locally named. More and more, however, Honshū archaeologists have been applying site names to Hokkaidō types. One disadvantage is a tendency to isolate these islands from Honshū, which, at least during certain stages of the Jōmon development, cannot be disassociated from the others. The thesis behind these five divisions is that the evolution throughout Japan is unilinear, or in other words, one in which each area passes through comparable stages in the evolution, including the finer degrees of pottery types within each stage. One result of this is the simplification of the problems of relationships within a given geographical area to primarily those of chronological sequences;

its value lies largely in the useful terminology it creates, but its idealism hardly compensates for its lack of realism. At present few Jōmonologists see it otherwise, but for early types at least, there is adequate evidence that parallel evolutions due to concentrations of certain types in small localities did occur.[5] Thus, as strict sequential chronologies make for neat terminologies, this description of Jōmon prehistory, to be coherent, will follow the abbreviated one given below. These names are taken mainly from the more detailed pottery sequence in the Kantō because of their universal familiarity, but their use is in no way intended to imply a belief in co-ordinated developments throughout Japan. They stand as symbols of levels of achievement.

EARLIEST	{ Inaridai–Tado { Kayama	*c.* 4500–3700 B.C.
EARLY	{ Hanazumi { Sekiyama–Kurohama { Moroiso	*c.* 3700–3000 B.C.
MIDDLE	{ Katsusaka { Ubayama	*c.* 3000–2000 B.C.
LATE	{ Horinouchi { Kasori	*c.* 2000–1000 B.C.
LATEST	Angyo (or Kamegaoka in Tōhoku)	*c.* 1000–250 B.C. (in south Japan)

For those who have some trinitarianism in their blood, Earliest and Early merely become Early, Middle remains the same, and Late and Latest are combined as simply Late. The approximate dating is based on three known $C14$ dates, one only published so far. Obviously these dates can be considered as only tentative, the round numbers doing nothing more than emphasizing the approximations.

Jōmon man lived near the sea coast and earned his subsist-
ence by gathering and eating shell-fish. Sea-shells of greater
abundance were preferred in the early stages, though as time
progressed there was a ready switch to fresh-water shells as they
became more accessible. The mountain dwellers, equally as
early in time as the first shell collectors, congregated in small
communities, hunted game and lived on fruits, nuts, berries
and edible roots.

THE SITES

Shell-mounds, or more descriptively for Japan, kitchen-
middens, since they are always flush with the surface of the
land, are concentrated along the protected bays of the east
coast. Warm-water currents washing these inlets produced
natural breeding conditions for shell-fish, and Jōmon people
soon discovered where their most prolific sources were. By a
recent count about 2,000 middens have been discovered, with
the greatest density in the Tokyo Bay region and along rivers
of the Kantō Plain, and only slightly less concentrated in the
bays of Matsushima and Ishinomaki in the Tōhoku, the Atsumi
Bay of Shizuoka and Aichi, and Kojima Bay in the Inland
Sea at the constriction between Okayama and Kagawa prefectures. Hiroshima Bay has its measure, and the bays on the
west side of Kyūshū, particularly Ariake and Shimabara of
Kumamoto, also have their share. Mounds are not limited to
these concentrations by any means; a rare few may even be seen
on the west side of Honshū, and Hokkaidō possesses them on
all four shores, though in greatest quantity along the coastlines
of its crooked leg and foot. Often one finds the mounds are
clustered like a small community; the Kamihongo mounds,
Chiba, which totalled nine or more by some counts, yielded
Ubayama (Middle Jōmon) pottery and therefore must be of
the same time-period.

The Kantō Plain has been rising throughout most of the Jōmon period and later centuries, and in places there is a wide strip of land between the mounds and the water's edge quite devoid of prehistoric remains. This fact combined with the realization that a number of mounds show a transition from salt-water to fresh-water shells in lower to upper levels that demonstrates continued habitation of the area as marine shells lost their accessibility and riverine shells became the nearest food source, provided the clue which broke the impasse in attempts to construct chronologies and give relative dates to mounds in the Plain. Ōyama worked out the method: it is simply that the mounds the most distant from the ocean and composed chiefly of marine shells are the oldest, and inversely, those nearest the modern coastline and consisting largely of riverine shells are the most recent.[6] When applied specifically, the relative ages of a number of mounds in a group may be determined. While all of this is feasible in the Kantō due to the multitude of mounds and the changing topographical conditions that include rivers finding new courses and the receding ocean, the use of this method has not been possible elsewhere in Japan. In addition, once the chronology of pottery types was established, archaeologists no longer needed such a cumbersome crutch. In this respect, Sakazume's study of 541 mounds of the Kantō district reveals that many of the smaller ones contain only one pottery type; larger ones, logically enough, range from three types and up. Examples would include Anjikidaira 3; Kasori 4; Ubayama 4; Ōmori 5; Natsushima 5; Shimpukuji 6; and Yoshii 9.[7]

Kantō Plain shell-mounds on the modern map extend towards Ōmiya (Ibaragi) in the north, to Sano in the north-west, and to approximately Tokorozawa in the west; they exist in the Boso and Miura Peninsulas, although the former has surprisingly few. These mounds are especially concentrated around the Kitaura and Kasumigaura Lakes; along the

Map 1

tributaries or old beds of the Edo River; the Ara River and nearer the bay, the Sumida River; and by the Tama River. Not far from the ancient coast they are plentiful on the Tokyo Bay side of the Miura Peninsula, and lie on a line from Yokohama that follows the train route through Ōmori, along the Yamate Line tracks towards Kawaguchi, then skirts the eastern part of Tokyo city, moving across to Ichikawa city and Chiba. The eastern coast of the Boso Peninsula and the Ibaragi seaboard are peculiarly bare. By drawing lines to connect the mounds that are the closest to today's shore, a quite different picture of the Jōmon period coastline materializes. The eastern part of Tokyo city, for instance, is mostly new land, unavail-able for habitation during prehistoric times. The two large lakes in Chiba were part of wide inlets; these lakes, Imba and Tega, now feed the Tonegawa. Somewhat similar topo-graphical conditions prevailed in the hinterland of Sendai Bay, though on a less spectacular scale. The Kitakami Plain is of recent formation, and lakes were stranded as the water receded. Shell-mounds are disposed along this plain and many are also hard by the coastline, and scattered among the islands of the bays of Matsushima and Ishinomaki. On a still smaller scale, near Hachinohe in Aomori and along the banks of Ogara Lake, the prehistoric inlets were shelters for shell-fish eaters in fertile shell breeding grounds. In other bays, usually on the warmer east side, this situation repeats itself.

Of the bivalve mussels, the *Meretrix meretrix*, the Japanese *Hamaguri* that enjoys much popularity today, and the *Ostrea gigas*, an oyster, are particularly common. Munro reached the conclusion that the criterion for edibility must have been whether they opened on boiling; if not they were discarded without further ado.[8] Two shells which are vital in aiding an understanding of chronology of the Jōmon period are the *Anadara granosa*, a warm water shell, and the *Pecten yesoensis*, a cold water marine shell. As the climate along the Pacific

Map 1   Shell-mounds in the Kantō Plain

coast cooled, the former moved south and began to disappear in the upper layers of mounds in the Kantō. In earliest prehistoric times it was habitually gathered for food along the northern coast of Honshū, but is today rare even as far north as Tokyo Bay. As it diminishes with time in the Jōmon period in the north, it sheds some light on the age of the mounds in which it is found. The opposite is the case with the *Pecten yesoensis*, now seen along the east Pacific coast north of Tokyo Bay and along the north-west coast of Honshū. It moved down during the Jōmon period and later. Sometimes the two are found together in the same mound, as at Miyatojima near Sendai. This would seem to be an indication that Jōmon man lived in a warmer climate, sub-tropical at least in South Japan, although the shells from the shell-mounds of Kyūshū itself are little different from those picked up for their food value today.

These shell-heaps are the most complete repository of Neolithic remains in Japan. Not only did the kitchen refuse accumulate, but broken and unusable objects were discarded there, burials were frequently cut right into them, and pits of dwellings located below them. Because of the chemical content of the shells, bones may be prevented from disintegration, and conversely, burials are exceedingly rare discoveries outside a shell-mound context. It should be added that although the shell-mounds are extremely important storehouses of Neolithic artifacts, in actual fact they make up only a small percentage of all Jōmon period sites. The very nature of the shell-mound furnishes the ingredients of stratigraphy: earth mixed with shells for the top-most level, shells and foreign debris in the middle, and shells mixed with earth for the lowest level, in the simplest of middens. Shells rarely descend to a depth of more than 4 feet in level territory, although the thickness of the bed depends on the slope of the terrain in some instances. Under such topographical conditions, the amassing of shells to a depth of 20 feet has been recorded. There are cases, as at the immense Kasori midden, where layers of earth or ash indicate that the makers of the heap either by force or volition abandoned the area, only to return themselves later or to have someone else take over the spot. Movements of this kind may, of course, be due to seasonal food supplies, and are phenomena that are

Fig. 2

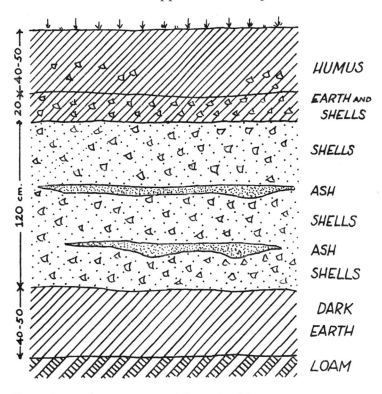

HUMUS

EARTH AND SHELLS

SHELLS

ASH

SHELLS

ASH

SHELLS

DARK EARTH

LOAM

Fig. 2   Section of Loc. CI, Kasori shell-mound, Chiba

invaluable from the viewpoint of the archaeologist's interest in succession of artifact types. The Kasori mound also repre-sents the enormous size that Kantō mounds may assume; resembling a figure 8, from north to south it stretches over 1,200 feet, from east to west approximately 600. No vertical sequence of pottery types was noted in the 1936 excavation, but the midden has given its name to non-successive types from two of the locations that were dug: Kasori E and Kasori B.

It is not uncommon to find the pits of dwellings below the level of shells in a midden or occasionally near by, but since there may be no leads to guide the digging in adjacent areas, the actual position of the houses and their relationship to the mound are not always certain. In many instances the population must have resided to the south, perhaps to avoid as far as possible the noxious odours that would have made the humid summer days most unbearable, as Munro suggested.[9] A number of years ago on warm summer days the author observed the excavation of a shell-mound situated near manure wells, and realized that this suggestion was a most pungent one.

In the shell bed, and frequently in a lower earth layer but preserved because of proximity to the shells, burials are often discovered. Skeletons in a shell stratum must have been intentionally deposited after a shallow pit had been scraped out amongst the shells, even though the task would have been arduous and unpleasant, and these burials rate as late arrivals; but those interred below the shell layer, and the hollowed out pits for dwellings also under the shell bed may be contemporary with the early stages of the accumulation of the mound or, as is sometimes believed, are the remains of a somewhat earlier occupation. When the shell bed is in direct contact with the pit-dwelling floor the evidence points to the beginning of the formation of the midden immediately after the abandonment of the house. Moves must have taken place for any number of reasons, but the impression is sometimes given that the mounds overtook the residences like an unstemmable tide, and houses were moved out of temporary reach of the encroaching menace.

For at least a large part of the year the early inhabitants lived semi-subterraneanly. This was particularly necessary in the colder climate of Tōhoku and Hokkaidō, and a considerable number of dwellings have been located in these regions, with undoubtedly more to come after further investigation. In the Kantō and Chūbu mountains it was customary to live in this manner. The typical pit hollowed out for protection was between 15 and 17 feet in length and nearly as wide, dug to a level floor deeper than 2 feet below the ground surface. Four or more upright posts were inserted in the ground across which four or more beams were laid, and then poles slanted in from all sides produced the needed support for a ridge pole placed

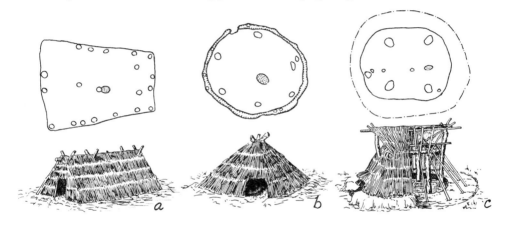

Fig. 3   Reconstructed pit-dwellings: (a) rectangular Jōmon type, (b) circular Jōmon type, (c) Yayoi type

along the top. These were all lashed together and covered with bark or leaves, and in some cases, earth. A ramp led to a doorway, a simple hole in earlier dwellings, but specially made with the aid of two posts and a projecting roof, appropriately ditched, in later ones. Often the greater the refinement of the doorway, the more recent is the house. Some floors were paved with large smooth stones, an improvement much preferred in more mountainous areas, and dwellings from Middle Jōmon on have some sort of fireplace near the centre. Middle Jōmon pit-dwellings are the most plentiful, frequently found in groups of fifteen or more, representing small to moderate sized communities.

Only a few are known from the Earliest Jōmon stage, not necessarily so much due to a warmer climate, but because the remains of a smaller population are sparse, and extensive ground digging implements were not very satisfactory. In Ōita prefecture at Hayamizudai a pit approximately 15 feet square must belong to a very early date. During Kayama times in the Kantō the dwellings were roughly square with rounded corners, and had not yet been graced with a hearth. Pits first

Fig. 3b

became round in the Moroiso period, but many home owners retained the more traditional shape. The rectangular Early

Fig. 3a

Jōmon pits vary quite considerably in number of post-holes; these may range anywhere from twenty to forty. The longer buildings were sometimes enlarged at intervals when emergencies or family increase required it. Pit D of Group B at Fukuoka village, Iruma county, Saitama, one of the largest dwellings known that measures 24½ feet by 19½ feet and has a complicated arrangement of ditches and holes, must have been lengthened seven times, judging partly by the removal of the fireplaces. Of other examples, one in the Shimaibata shell-mound, Itabashi ward of Tokyo city, only 14¾ feet by 14 feet in size, whose pottery types (Hanazumi, Sekiyama and Moroiso) are all Early Jōmon, was expanded four times. It has nine hearths of various shapes. Obviously this means that the rectangular form of many is not a part of the original plan. A rare few Early period houses seem to have had wooden shelves supported by slender props. The relatively infrequent early fireplaces are oval in shape, formed of stones, often to the west of centre in the house. Quadrangular houses normally have an east–west orientation.

The Middle Jōmon communities of the central and western side of the Plain, and those that made up the clusters of population in the central mountains must have been organized into rather efficient bands for hunting, fishing, collecting, and possibly for defence if the need arose. The majority are located near advantageous water sources on plateaus overlooking rivers, yet one of the Kusabana pits, Nishi-tama county, Greater Tokyo, is so far from its water source, the Hirai River, that it must have been pathetically inconvenient. One therefore thinks of something along the order of a parturition house or ostracization rather than free choice.

A glance at several of the classic representatives of Middle Jōmon villages will give a comprehensive cross-section of the archaeological record. At the Ubayama shell-mound six different pit types were noted, and since they are almost all on the same level, and by the pottery yard-stick all belong to about the same period, there must have been considerable flexibility and personal preference in house design. There is little to suggest that social status, size of family or time differences would have been responsible for this. These shapes run the series from oval through square and rectangular, with irregularities and rounded corners. The most striking discovery was five skeletons on the floor of one pit, Location B, Pit 1, not in the usual neat burial manner, but in complete disarray that could only have come about by violent action. Of these, two were male adults, three female adults and one a child. Barring the possibility that a party to which neighbours were invited was in progress, and including the chance that mass murder may have been committed, this particular residence has been taken as illustrating the average space needed by a family of five. With this size as a point of departure, 13 feet by $11\frac{1}{2}$ feet and 2 feet 5 inches deep, complicated computations have been made to get a rough idea of how many mouths a community had to feed. Though recognizing the overwhelming number of 'ifs', the hypothesis is interesting to toy with. This house may have fallen with greater gusto than most; there are no markings for the usual slender poles that would carry the roof to the ground, and it may therefore have been of unusual design, and one might add, even top-heavy. The architectural genius of the Middle Jōmon period, however, was the inventor of the house without centre pole; the fireplace could go where it logically belonged, and precious space was freed for more efficient use. Some of the dwellings of Ubayama face south, and the entrance-ways are ditched and marked by post-holes. In the south-west corner of one dwelling a hole about 3 feet across contained a jar and skull of a dog. This house also seems to have had a roof which did not reach the ground.

Middle Jōmon people, capable of making pottery vessels of huge scale, also were the first to use jars for hearths. Sometimes these were complete jars; at other times either the upper or lower part was used, often open at the bottom. Stones for the fireplace pit were still employed, but another novelty at this time was an oval-shaped shaft lined with large and varied potsherds. There is no question but that these fragments were already broken when arranged in place. The jar hearths are common at Ubayama. The excavation of a hearth below floor level at Hiromi, Nagano, revealed a fine Katsusaka style vessel surrounded on three sides by long stone slabs.

Plate 1

A perplexing problem is created by those stone or jar arrangements that resemble fireplaces yet contain no traces whatsoever of cooking or heating. In a few cases these formations are not clearly associated with dwellings, and they may therefore be outdoor storage pits, or perhaps something along the order of offering places. The suggestion of an unfinished house could also be made, and the fact that two of the dwelling pits at Kusabana contained fireplaces which appeared not to have been used does not aid in the solution of the problem. Pit-dwelling 3 had a stone paved depression 32 inches across and 16 deep over which had been piled a great heap of stones. Charcoal remains between the stone pile and flooring led the excavators to believe that this may have been used like a steam bath, but in another case where a pottery jar was sunk in the middle with stone paving built around it, and over 400 stones by count were amassed, there were no signs to indicate its purpose.

The simple shaft-type fireplace was used at Kusabana. Charcoal from *Quercus serrata*, a kind of oak, was found in this kind of hearth in Pit-dwelling 2, showing that Jōmon people already had a prototype of the modern-day *hibachi*, the charcoal urn heater. Some of the houses here had more than one fireplace, probably in contemporary use. A ditch by this same residence may have been used as a storage well for edible tubers (*imo*), but the Kusabana houses are mostly deeply trenched for water control, although intersecting ditches presented insoluble problems to the archaeologists; the ditches may belong to different dates.

Stone floors, popular in Middle and Late Jōmon, were usually constructed of smooth river rocks. Some are so neatly fitted together that there seems to have been no space for post-holes. People living mostly in Greater Tokyo, Kanagawa, Yamanashi, Shizuoka, Nagano and Gumma chose the cold stone over the damp earth, and many laid the stones very skilfully in wall-to-wall paving. Late Jōmon people may have covered their floors with mats.

Nagano's greatest Middle Jōmon sites are Togaruishi, Yosukeone and Hiraide. Togaruishi (Toyohira village, Suwa county) is ideally situated on a plateau of the Yatsugatake's west slope at an elevation of approximately 3,400 feet. Springs are near by in adjoining valleys. The community constituted a minimum of sixty houses, as that many have been uncovered, but it was probably three times that size, and must have spanned many centuries of the third millennium B.C. One house had a pit near its hearth that contained remains of enough red pigment to have been used as a storage container for paint. Paint of this type was sometimes used for pottery decoration.

Yosukeone is on the opposite side of the mountain. Over thirty dwellings run the gamut of round pits with many posts, more or less square, and square with rounded corners and four posts. In the round houses the customary hearth was a jar sunk into the ground; the shaft-type hearth corresponded generally with the squarish dwelling pits, and the stone-lined and enclosed fireplace with the four-posted house. The excavator believed these changes were largely chronological. This community was more consistent in religious practices than most, for in the north-west corner of a great majority of the houses stood a stone platform, one or more stone pillars, where were deposited stone clubs of a phallic nature, clay figurines and potsherds.

Fig. 16

The community of Hiraide, at Sōga village, Higashi-chikuma county, was dispersed across a terrace that measured close to 1,100 yards east–west and 440 north–south, near the Narai River. A spring at the south-west corner of the village is still flowing steadily today, adequate for the needs of the present farming population. Excavations were conducted here inter-mittently from 1947 to 1953. Almost continuous occupation from the third millennium B.C. to modern times makes Hiraide of particular interest to those concerned with the evolution of community life in Japan. Middle Jōmon people left traces of seventeen semi-subterranean dwellings; Late Jōmon potsherds (Horinouchi type of zoned cord-impressed) number only a few; and the Yayoi transition, to judge by the quantity of pottery, was brief and insignificant; but Haji iron users of the protohistoric era and perhaps later accounted for forty-nine pit-dwellings and other structures. Glazed pottery, brought in from the Kansai probably, was the property of Nara and Heian period residents whose tenancy continued well into the tenth century A.D.

Most of the Jōmon period houses were circular, had four or more supporting pillars for the slanting roofs, and a jar or stone arrangement for a fireplace slightly off-centre to the north or west. In dwellings F, I and J many pieces of pottery were profusely strewn on the floor around the centre of the pit, and in I and J a considerable number were large sized vessels complete or only partially broken. These accumulations are a phenomenon that has not yet been satisfactorily explained. Several of the pieces from I are so similar they could have been made by one potter. Fragments of five clay figurines, all that were found except a human-faced handle discovered in dwelling F, were in hut H, a house that was destroyed by fire. Chunks of charred posts were *in situ*, and pieces of clay had been rebaked by the heat. The size of the house, or any of its features for that matter, do not distinguish it from the others.

Pit-dwellings of late stages of Jōmon centuries are almost as elusive as surface-dwellings. The latter must have been constructed throughout most of the Jōmon period—the Ubayama shell-mound seems to have had at least one—but became increasingly popular, not due to a more tolerable climate, but to improved building methods that stimulated the changing style. The semi-subterranean type was less needed now that houses were more secure, better insulated and ventilated, yet they were nevertheless often constructed by Yayoi builders. A late Jōmon one was found in the Ohata shell-mound, Shizuoka, rounded in shape, with eight post-holes in a circle. A 3-foot-wide embankment of stones surrounded the house in an outline that was more or less square, rounded at the corners. It formed a sort of dike, and is the earliest instance of the use of stones to control the flow of water. Angyo stage dwelling pits are square or quadrangular, small and shallow, 6 or 7 feet across, or may even reach the other extreme, like the 33-foot rectangular one of the Shimpukuji shell-mound. These almost all have flagstone floors, a feature that was carried on by Yayoi successors.

Deer (*Cervus nippon nippon* Temminck) and wild boar (*Sus leucomystax leucomystax* Temminck & Schlegel) roamed the mountains and plains of Japan and were to Jōmon people the most highly prized game. Remains of these animals are profusely scattered in many shell-mounds, particularly in Middle and Late periods, and the long bones were split to remove the marrow and in some cases made into useful tools. Antlers of deer are frequently found cut so that the tine forms a pick, like the Lyngby axe of Mesolithic Denmark. The boar supplied fat for oil, the deer fur for winter clothing. Smaller animals called for trapping skill with fewer rewards, but for seasonal variation the badger, raccoon dog and hare were eaten and their fur utilized.

Fig. 4

Stone missile points, more or less triangular in shape with convex base, were used by the Earliest Jōmon hunters, and in succeeding centuries shapes were variable and all types were in contemporary use. After Middle Jōmon some were worked in bone, but it was a Horinouchi stone worker who first chipped out the tanged arrowhead and tipped a bow with bone pieces. The finest arrowheads are of obsidian, smaller in later periods, and more plentiful nearer the sources of raw material. Bows were in use throughout the Jōmon period, but in only very late sites have their remains been discovered. Five were found in the peat bed at Korekawa in Aomori. Fragments show that all were more than 40 inches in length, and the complete one

Fig. 5b

measured 48 inches and was composed of two strips of *crypto-meria* (Japanese cedar) bound together by ribbons of bark; it still bore traces of red lacquer. The longest was 68 inches.

Wild birds made an occasional delicacy, but the general scarcity of their remains suggests that the means of shooting and trapping them left much to be desired. Ducks, geese, kites, pheasants, cranes and a few others found their way into the family pot.

The vast majority of fish bones in the mounds belong to those which could be easily caught in the inlets especially at high tide; these include perch, mullet, gilthead, snapper, dragonet and some sea-bream, but remains of deep-sea fish, like the tunny, shark, sting-ray, and even the whale, attest to the extreme antiquity of the widespread fishing industry. Also, a small percentage of shells from some mounds are those whose habitat ranges from 30 to 120 feet in water depth.

Bone fish-hooks and harpoons are not uncommon in mounds of the Kantō and around Sendai. The former are rare in Earliest Jōmon mounds and strangely enough are virtually non-existent in the entire Hanazumi, Sekiyama and Moroiso stages of Early Jōmon, but become more and more plentiful in Katsusaka and later. Harpoons were not invented until Middle Jōmon, at about which time the dugout canoe came into common use probably because the improved wood-working tools that the Katsusaka people devised for their extensive house-building programme made the task of hollowing out a log far simpler. Long and multi-barbed harpoons show that Late Jōmon man ventured farther to sea. The longest of these harpoons have as many as five pairs of barbs, and ones with fewer barbs may be long and lance-like or curved. Spear points represent other means of killing fish, and ray-fish tail-spikes were made use of as needles. Salmon abounded in North Japanese rivers and along the coast; today they spawn as far south as the Tone River. Toward the end of the Neolithic they were undoubtedly one of the principal sources of food for northern people, and thus became the subject-matter for stone engravings. In a way that suggests a kind of fetish, these carvings may be seen on a number of stones in the Tōhoku area. Six have been discovered, the most elaborate ones appearing on a stone in the town of Yajima, Akita, as twelve simply

Plate 4

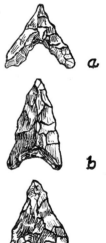

a

b

c

Fig. 4 Arrowheads of the Jōmon period: (a) Ōgura, Kyōto, (b) I. C. U., Tokyo, $\frac{15}{16}''$, (c) Tera, Nagano

Plate 33

incised salmon of differing but nearly half sizes, pointed in varying directions and sometimes overlapping. These are dated only tentatively by the Jōmon pottery found near by.

The house dog, gravitating naturally towards habitations, appeared on the scene early and multiplied rapidly; he may have been trained for hunting, and certainly acted as a watchdog and house pet. Numerous remains have been found; for instance in the Yoshigo midden, Aichi, in a location where thirty-three human skeletons were recovered, bones of ten dogs (three male, seven female) were also brought to light. As early as the Hanazumi stage of Early Jōmon at the type-site shell-mound near Toyoharu village, Saitama, bones of the *Canis familiaris japonicus* Temminck, the small dog that has evolved into the modern Shiba, were found in twenty places. A Hori-nouchi date dog-lover buried his best friend in an oval-shaped pit 32 inches by 16 inches directly under the shell layer of Nishiga-yato mound, Yokohama. Archaeologists found the skeleton per-fectly preserved. Yet at Ubayama special burials were not given, and scratches on several bones may even have been made in the process of scraping off the animals' flesh. If this was for food, one can interpret it only in terms of dire economic conditions.

Cats were wild; a cranium from the Early Jōmon Nojima shell-mound, Kanagawa, and a lower jaw of one from Ichiōji shell-mound, Aomori, both belong to the wild cat, like those of Korea and Tsushima. These may be the ancestors of the tame Honshū cats because of their similarity, yet it is quite possible that domesticated cats were all imported, as is often believed. The pig was brought in later from China, and never reached the main Japanese islands in Jōmon times, but it is known in Ryūkyū Island sites.

Although the belief is generally held that the horse was introduced by Yayoi people, its appearance in Jōmon sites that precede Yayoi times by too great a span would seem to disprove the assumption. The Yayoi people were possibly horse riders who brought their steeds with them, but their needs for the horse were quite limited and their dependence on it is not borne out by illustrations on bronze bells and pottery. Its representation does not appear until the Tomb period when its popularity is clearly recognized in the clay effigies, wall paintings in tombs, and metal engravings. At the Ataka mound, Kumamoto, Kyūshū, in a pottery context that could hardly be later than Middle Jōmon, bones of the small horse were found. The bones from Izumi, Kagoshima, would be only slightly more recent. Later, and belonging to Angyo and Kamegaoka stages or their equivalent, at the mounds of Homi, Aichi; Kozahara, Nagano; Ōbora, Miyagi; Azusawa, Tokyo; horse bones may actually have a relationship to the more mobile Yayoi culture entering South Japan. Those found at Ōbora were considered to have no characteristics which would distinguish them from the modern horse. The majority of Jōmon horses were small, not unlike the Tokara pony, and cared for until they died of old age. The bones are never found mutilated. Small Yayoi period horses come from Tayui, Nagasaki, and Urigo, Aichi, but Yayoi horses are generally somewhat larger, average thirteen hands, and are more like Korean Stone Age horses. Classified as medium-sized horses, it seems to be no accident that as a rule the further the Yayoi horse from the Korean peninsula the larger he was. The small horse retained its strain throughout the pre-Buddhist era, however, for the Hiraide horse of the Haji period was a small one quite comparable to his Jōmon ancestor.

Contacts with the incoming Yayoi culture no doubt contributed towards the further realization of the Neolithic nature of this prehistoric period. One result of these contacts may have been cattle breeding which is indicated at the Okadaira shell-mound in Ibaragi and at Homi on the Atsumi Peninsula in Aichi, in the remains of the domestic short-horned cow.

Wild vegetables and fruit of the order of the wild grape were

Fig. 5 Wooden sword and bow from Kore-kawa, Aomori: (a) 24", (b) 48"

gathered in season. However, the very existence of the communities, the stone implements suitable for cultivation, and pottery usable for the storage of foods are all indications of a society at least partially dependent on agriculture after Middle Jōmon times. Chestnuts and walnuts would have been an inducement for inhabitants to remain more stationary, and vegetables on a small scale were most likely raised. Only in late periods, however, is there certain indication in the remains from sites that some cultivation took place. Barnyard millet was grown in isolated places; buckwheat, sesame seed and the hairy-podded kidney bean in other instances, the last three found in the peat layer of the Shimpukuji shell-mound, Saitama. Hemp was discovered directly under the shell layer at the Yoyama mound, Chiba. While these may have been developed eventually on a much broader scale, it took the introduction of rice into Kyūshū to change the economy of the country drastically.

The wealth of preserved woods at Korekawa furnishes a cross-section of those considered useful for various needs. They include wood of the following trees: chestnut, elm, cypress, birch, cherry and fir.

TOOLS AND POTTERY

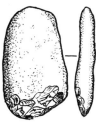

Fig. 6 Pebble tool from Kozanji shell-mound, Wakayama

Any smooth stones used by Earliest Jōmon man were nature-formed and found by river banks. In some cases hand-sized ones of oval shape were chipped on one edge to be usable as chopping tools, or chipped stone axes of somewhat similar shape were slightly polished on one bevelled edge. Almost any available material was used for the rough implements providing it was sturdy enough: sandstone, andesite, shale, quartzite, serpentine, schist, jasper, basalt and obsidian; and for the polished tools argillite, diorite, ophiolite, jadeite, and several of those just mentioned. The more sedentary Middle Jōmon populations had flat stone mortars of oval or rectangular outline, sometimes four-legged and with a raised rim. Spherical grinding stones were used with these. Pitted stones give

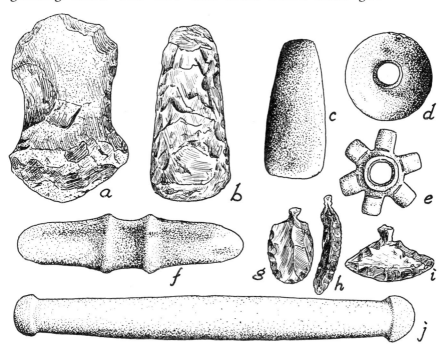

Fig. 7   Stone implements of the Jōmon period: (a, d, f) Horinouchi shell-mound, Chiba, (b) Chojagahara, Niigata, (c) Ubayama shell-mound, Chiba, (g-i) Kamegaoka, Aomori; others uncertain

evidence of the friction needed for the making of fire, and in their ambitious building operations they utilized a rough rectangular or fiddle-shaped axe. Often these axes were fractured river rocks chipped all the way round but still retaining a smooth surface on one side. These were hafted to the short end of a tree joint and employed in the arts of digging and

Fig. 7a, b

Fig. 8

Fig. 8 Middle Jōmon period implement used as axe and digging tool

Fig. 7j

Fig. 7d, e

Fig. 7f

woodcutting. Present-day use of this type of stone implement may still be seen in the Caroline and Fiji Islands, and New Guinea. Polished axes, oval and rectangular in section, were in use in Middle and Late Jōmon, the latter finding greater favour in later periods. Grinding of the stone to produce a hand axe was introduced in Early Jōmon times; a great upsurge in the making of ground and polished stone implements took place right after the Middle Jōmon period, at which time with increased technical skill the production of clubs, mace-heads, axes, swords and other objects that were either magical or had a magical counterpart was dramatically spurred. The so-called stone club (*seki-bō*), unknown in pre-Katsusaka assemblages, is too consistently phallic in nature to have had its beginnings only as a small pestle for pulverizing wild grain and nuts, and the long ones that may reach 5 feet in length, are impractically heavy for normal use. The circular and spoked mace-heads had their origins in Horinouchi times; the latter began as three-lobed stones in the mountains at least. These may have served as hammers in the case of circular ones, or as a weapon in the hunt and even in human combat, and perhaps additionally in a ceremonial capacity. The double-ended grooved axe follows an evolution that has every appearance of a transformation from a useful to a magical object: some taper sharply toward the ends and are provided with a rather simple constriction in the middle with little or no emphasis on the separating ridge; others are long and slender, gracefully curved, and often considerably flattened along the edges, virtually forming thin and narrow blades or needle-like spikes. These flattened grooved axes more often than not come from the Tōhoku area and are tokens of Late Jōmon workmanship, but this type is also distributed throughout the Kantō, across the Tōsan into the Hokuriku. In rare instances the centre is perforated and the ridges enlarged, making the object look much like a mace-head with two extended spikes.

A purely quadrangular axe, chipped or polished, was intro/
duced in Middle Jōmon, but the polished variety is not an
implement of widespread use until Horinouchi times. There
are numerous variations on the fiddle/shaped digging and
cutting tool; one is plectrum/shaped, popular among mountain
dwellers. The prehistoric multiple/purpose tin/opener was a
tanged knife/scraper especially effective for opening shells,
cutting hides, peeling skins from and cutting up animals and
vegetables. This implement abounds in sites particularly in
North Japan and where obsidian, flint or silicates were more
available, but from one end of the islands to the other it proved
its worth. The northern ones through Middle Jōmon are
tanged on the long end, but then begin to take on a more tri/
angular shape, rather isosceles, in which the tang forms the apex.
Actually both kinds in many shapes were used. An occa/
sional one in North Japan will have two tangs. In some of the
earliest sites of Kyūshū the tangs are opposite the long cutting
edge like the later type in the north, and after Horinouchi all of
these knives disappear from the Kantō Plain. Drills and tang/
less knives served similar and other purposes. Needles, and
fish/hooks often ornamentally carved at the base in later times
in Tōhoku and Hokkaidō and infrequently lacquered and
polished, were produced from bone, horn or the ivory of tusks.

Fig. 7c

Fig. 7g–i

Bones and sharks' teeth were worked into arrowheads some/
times perforated at the base, with or without stem, and these
and stone ones were firmly affixed to the shaft with the aid of
resin. Laurel/leaf/shaped spear points were in continuous use
throughout the Jōmon period, although they tend to become
smaller, more slender and refined in the late stages; they may also
have a constriction near the end and be tanged. On the west
coast where peculiarities are almost habitual, one type of spear/
head is pointed at both ends and narrowed through the middle,
one head being larger than the heel.

Harpoons, hooks, stone and clay sinkers, and dugout boats

Fig. 9b

Fig. 9a

attest to the advanced means employed in harvesting sea food. The skull of a sea-bream from the Shiizuka shell-mound of Ibaragi with a bone point through its head is more graphic evidence of success than the bulk of the discards. Stone weights for attachment to nets are rounded or cylindrical, notched or grooved; clay weights, utilized more for sinkers of hook-and-line fishing, are fragments of pottery whose edges are rounded, smoothed and notched. The pottery type dates these with little difficulty, but some Jōmon sites have yielded circular discs in considerable numbers that resemble sinkers but have no notches, so may be pieces for some kind of game. The nets were of twisted fibres, and three- and four-armed stones were possibly the weights for the plaiting of the ropes, or were perhaps used as spindle whorls in a simple method of spinning.

Remains of dugout canoes complete the picture of how Jōmon fishers brought back their deep sea catches. Approximately sixty whole or partial canoes of pre- and early-Buddhistic times have been found; many of these are impossible to date because of the circumstances of the finds and the lack of related objects, but modifications made from time to time can occasionally be identified, if in no other way, through illustrations of boats on Yayoi artifacts and in the graphic arts of the Tomb period. Possibly one of the earliest and also best preserved canoes was found at Yokoshiba-chō, Chiba. It is simply hollowed out of the log of a type of walnut tree of over 15 feet, and although its own date is uncertain, it was found with Jōmon pottery of the Early stages. The bow and stern are slightly raised and rather angular in a way that is supposed to be more typical of the protohistoric period. By the Tomb age, however, if not already during the Yayoi period, outrigging could be attached to each side, and five or six paddlers was not unusual. The Kamo canoe, preserved in a peat layer, may be the oldest should it precede the Yokoshiba one, and is quite rounded in cross-section, but neither bow nor stern are preserved. It seems clear that two canoe types were in contemporary use for long periods. One was not unlike the canoe of the Ainu, sleek in its appearance with tapered bow and stern; the other had squarish ends and more vertical lines. Some were provided with built-in cross-seats, and Neolithic ones may have had long, longitudinal bench-like formations that were intended to support movable transverse boards for seats. Six paddles were discovered at Kamo; two were large with long blades and four small with narrow blades. In this case all were designed for free movement in paddling on alternate sides of the boat. Only a single small one was complete and it measured 4 feet 4½ inches in length.

Fig. 9   Clay disc and weight from I. C. U., Tokyo. Length of (a) 1 7/16″, other to scale

Plates 3, 5

Although woodworking may have been a craft of considerable achievement, and wooden tools undoubtedly had varied uses, few items of wood remain today. Without earlier examples that might cast light on their significance, the red painted wooden spatulas or daggers from Korekawa, frequently referred to as swords, pose unsolved questions. More than ten were found at a depth greater than 6 feet below the surface. They are of Japanese cedar and average 2 feet in length. All bear carved designs near the hilt, from which project two tangs perhaps for attachment to a handle. These objects seem to have followed no metal types in spite of the fact that they were made at a time that corresponded to the importation of metal in South Japan. Even facetiously they can hardly be called the prototypes of the modern Ainu moustache-lifter. What must unquestionably be a ceremonial sword was discovered in the same layer. In surprisingly fine condition, it is also of Japanese cedar, entirely red lacquered, and bears carving on the spherical pommel, the hand-guard and the knobbed end. It is only slightly longer than the wooden daggers. Red wooden combs also came from this site; they no longer have their teeth, which were long, and eight, ten or eleven in number. The frame is triangularly shaped and sometimes perforated. The combs

Fig. 5a

served more ornamental than practical purposes. Annular bracelets and pulley-shaped ear-rings of red lacquered wood came to light as well.

Impressed mat marks on the base of many Late Jōmon pottery vessels show that mat making and basketry was already an accomplished art. Some of these imprints are extremely neat and quite deep, and may have resulted from the stacking of pots within each other before firing. Over and above the wooden pieces already mentioned, the Korekawa swamp contained many wicker objects, twisted vine nets probably for

(1) *Kawasaki, Ōita, (2) Hitoyoshi, Kumamoto, (3) Nishino-omote, Kagoshima, (4) Ōguchi, Kagoshima, (5) Ibusuki, Kagoshima, (6) Kusano, Kagoshima, (7) Sakura-jima, Kagoshima, (8) Nishibira, Kumamoto, (9) Goryo, Kumamoto, (10) Yusu, Fukuoka, (11) Kozanji shell-mound, Wakayama, (12) Ishiyama shell-mound, Shiga, (13) Ishiyama shell-mound, Shiga, (14) Irimi shell-mound, Aichi, (15) Kitashirakawa, Kyōto, (16) Kitashirakawa, Kyōto, (17) Ushimado-machi, Okayama, (18) Kitashirakawa, Kyōto, (19) Kitashirakawa, Kyōto, (20) Fukuda, Okayama, (21) Nishio shell-mound, Aichi, (22) Miyatake, Nara, (23) Kashiwara, Nara, (24) Kasaoka city, Okayama, (25) Daimaru, Yokohama city, Kanagawa–Inaridai type, (26) Shirogadai shell-mound, Chiba–Tado Lower type, (27) Tobinodai, Chiba–Kayama type, (28) Nikki shell-mound, Chiba–Sekiyama type, (29) Orimoto shell-mound, Tsuda, Kanagawa–Moroiso type, (30) Orimoto shell-mound, Kanagawa–Moroiso type, (31) Narahara, Tokyo–Katsusaka type, (32) Togaruishi, Nagano–Katsusaka type, (33) Narahara, Tokyo–Ubayama (Kasori E) type, (34) Ubayama shell-mound, Chiba–Ubayama (Kasori E) type, (35) Horinouchi shell-mound, Chiba–Horinouchi type, (36) Naga-monoyama shell-mound, Chiba–Horinouchi type, (37–8) Kasori shell-mound, Chiba–Horinouchi (Kasori B) type, (39) Hirohata, Ibaragi–Horinouchi (Kasori B) type, (40) Tobe, Chiba–Omori type, (41) Okadaira shell-mound, Ibaragi–Kasori (Kasori B) type, (42) Shimpukuji shell-mound, Saitama–Angyo type, (43) Azusawa, Tokyo–Angyo type, (44) Itakura Lake, Gumma–Angyo type, (45) Hosokubo, Toyama, (46) Hijiyama, Gifu, (47) Hosokubo, Toyama, (48) Okayamaruyama, Nagano, (49) Asahi shell-mound, Himi city, Toyama, (50) Sekihara, Niigata, (51) Ogaya city, Nagano, (52) Inatomi, Nagano, (53) Kuwanagawa, Nagano, (54) Kuwanagawa, Nagano, (55) Sado Island, Niigata, (56) Sanō, Nagano, (57) Higashiware, Toyama, (58) Sanō, Nagano, (59) Fukirizawa, Aomori, (61) Enokibayashi, Aomori, (62) Fukura, Yamagata, (63) Korekawa, Aomori, (64) Daigi, Miyagi, (65) Ōyu, Akita, (66) Ōyu, Akita, (67) Ōyu, Akita, (68) Akita city, Akita, (69) Kamegaoka, Aomori, (70) Kamegaoka, Aomori, (71) Aso, Akita, (72) Kamegaoka, Aomori*

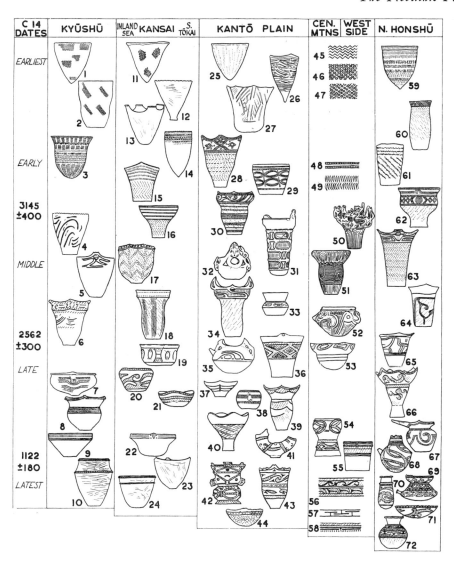

C 14 DATES	KYŪSHŪ	INLAND SEA KANSAI S. TŌKAI	KANTŌ PLAIN	CEN. MTNS	WEST SIDE	N. HONSHŪ

Fig. 10 Chart of Jōmon Pottery (Kantō Plain type names are given as a guide).
The dates are B.C. For key see opposite page

supporting pottery vessels potted in a wicker basket, plant fibres knitted into some sort of a covering, carved and ornamented tree forks of uncertain use, wooden bowls and cups on pedestals. The bark of birch, cherry, cedar and cypress was used. One circular basket with inturned rim and slightly pointed feet was constructed of sliced and woven fibres and then covered with a thick coating of red lacquer. A lacquered wooden container from the Shimpukuji shell-mound, Saitama, is probably just a little earlier in time.

The ceramic art of Neolithic Japan is one of great variety, of wide latitude in skill and broad fluctuations in taste. Its local changes, the chronological innovations and the inter-regional influences that cut in obliquely result in fine shades of deviation from main types in all areas, and have joined forces to enrich a craft with infinite degrees of quality and beauty. The probability remains that most households had a potter, and taking into consideration the endless amount of variations that are possible in the production of a vessel, it is not surprising to find so little uniformity; rather, it is more surprising perhaps that the archaeologist can retroactively fix acceptable norms for classifications.

Cord-impressing was used to embellish the surface of an overwhelming percentage of Neolithic pottery; its changes passed from its primitive inception when it was applied vertically by *Fig. 10 (25)* single cords or string rather than by plaited fibres, and widely spaced; through a stage in which the cords were twisted and *Fig. 10 (28)* rolled to produce a herring-bone effect, the Early Jōmon; then the Middle Jōmon period of bold and consistent diagonal appli- *Fig. 10 (34)* cation; and finally, as a style that permeated all corners of Japan in the Late Jōmon, it was done either obliquely or in short rotations multi-directionally and enclosed within lines by erasing *Fig. 10 (36 and others)* whatever had spilled over. This last is termed 'erased cord-impression' (*surikeshijōmon*) in Japanese; it will be referred to here as zoned cord-impressing. While these stages are successive, they are not necessarily so throughout the country: cord-marking is negligible in Kyūshū before Late Jōmon; no other area except the Kantō really goes through the throes of string-impressing; and during Middle Jōmon in the central mountains and on the west side—a region where rouletting, stick-marking, plain and sculptured surfaces were normally preferred—cord-marking was largely ignored. In some areas the standard methods of cord-marking were almost always accepted, but in others, like the Tōhoku in the Early period, although a standardized type does exist and could have provided the model, numerous experimental and unusual ways of using this technique were devised.

The earliest mode of pottery decoration dominant in South Japan was the use of a carved stick rolled over the wet clay surface. This, here termed rouletting, was applied to pointed-bottomed vessels in Kyūshū and perpetuated itself in that centre after pottery makers had discovered how to attach flat bottoms to their vessels, but in the Kansai, central mountains and west side, and in the relatively few sites of the Kantō where it is found, it does not outlive the pointed bottoms. A 1956 discovery in Hokkaidō, and later finds at Hachinohe, Aomori, and elsewhere in the Tōhoku have extended the distribution of this decoration far beyond previous expectation, though certainly not lessening its character as a southern technique. As it filtered into the Plain it also moved inland. Zigzags are the earliest and most prolific pattern, but ovals, lozenges, checks and others add variety. Contemporary with it in North Honshu is shell-imprinted and marked pottery, and early forms of cord-impressing. Shell-stamping is actually rather widespread, seen in South-west Kyūshū and the Kansai particularly. Most of the early types in the Kantō, including the Sekiyama-Kurohama stage of Early Jōmon, are fibre-tempered; in the north the change from fibre- to sand-tempering takes place during the time the cylindrical (*entō*) vessels are in production.

While string-impressing is evolving into fully fledged cord-impressing in the Kantō, lined and grooved types progress from

Fig. 10 (1, 2)

Plate 13

Fig. 10 (26, 27)

Fig. 10 (28)

pointed into rounded bottoms. The chief of these are Tado and Kayama. With the advent of Sekiyama and the consistent use of feather-shaped cord-impression to cover the lower two-thirds of a vessel's surface, a method of incising with a split bamboo stick in parallel lines and circular indentations was developing. This leads into the Moroiso stage, aspects of which may be seen in southern Tōhoku, the Tōsan and in the Kansai where they are known as Kitashirakawa types after the name of the Kyōto city site. Marking by the end of a bamboo stick, or perhaps even a finger-nail in many cases, is the most characteristic feature of the Early Jōmon period from the Chūgoku into the Tōhoku. In the Inland Sea punched marks appear in many different ways, but crescent patterns, at times made in a rocking motion, represent the ultimate unity that this style achieves, and coupled with it, for the first time serious attempts are made to decorate the vessels with applied clay. In the case of Moroiso

Fig. 10 (30)

this takes the form of simulated twisted rope patterns.

Fig. 10 (3)

Fig. 10 (4, 5)

Fig. 10 (6)

The Middle Jōmon of Kyūshū sees the continued use of grooving as the chief technique of decoration. It takes the form of short parallel lines in the nearly round-bottomed Sobata type of Early Jōmon. In Ataka these are lengthened into bold grooves of rather loose designs frequently spread across the entire surface and then reduced to tighter ones nearer the rim, though also not clearly organized. A heavy shell-imprinted rim is added to the Ichiki type, a type from shell-mounds that still retains some of the body grooving; its inland cognates carry narrower rims and are decorated by objects other than shells. The Middle Jōmon is less distinctive in the Chūgoku and Kansai, but in the Kantō and through the mountains it is most impressive, partly due to its sheer quantity. The major family groups are Katsusaka and Ubayama (Kasori E), with regional variations and subtypes known by other names. The earlier is usually ornamented with strips of clay applied to produce panels of decoration that take all shapes, the most common being horizontal oblongs. Cup-like inturned rims may be plain, or they may, like much of the rest of the surface, be covered with densely laid parallel clay strips often super- imposed and criss-crossed. Handles and rim projections add to the distorted silhouettes, and on the west coast where the heights of sculptural effects are reached, fantastic and asym- metrical protuberances completely obscure the neck and rim shape. The large Katsusaka jars can obviously double as cooking pots and heaters for hearths if need be. In this type the walls are thick, the clay is reddish and coarse.

In some instances heads of animals are absorbed into these massive projections. Rim-heads are more prevalent in the Tōsan, but are occasionally to be seen in the Plain. Most are now disassociated from their vessels, but in a rare case an intact one illustrates the possibilities of their position. They will be discussed later along with the significance of figurines in the Middle Jōmon period.

As the outburst of Katsusaka energy waned, the reaction swung towards exhaustive application of cord-impression, and the excesses of rim decoration were modified to two or four peaks. The neck and rim take most of the attached clay strips, now arranged in flowing curves, often spiralled. Variations and refinements of this Ubayama type are found throughout the Chūbu and into the lower Tōhoku, though its popularity diminishes progressively in the direction of the Kansai and Chūgoku. It already has the germs of zoned cord-impressing in it, and its successor, Horinouchi, the main bloc of the Late Jōmon period, witnesses the development and spread of this technique of decoration from Hokkaidō to Kyūshū. In the latter region its arrival took place after it was refined and when it was usual to limit it to narrow bands; in other areas it reaches this more sophisticated stage as time passes, and then is modified into lobe- or leaf-like patterns repeated around the surface. Con- temporary with these developments in zoned cord-impressing

Fig. 10 (31)

Plate 6; *Fig. 10 (51)*

Plate 7; *Fig. 10 (50)*

Fig. 10 (32)

Plate 8

Plate 10

Plates 9, 10

Plate 12

is decoration by parallel lines, often most elegantly handled. The spouted jar makes its début, in countless instances taking a globular form above and straight but sharply angled walls below. Rather high-arched loops are connected to the orifice in a saddle-shaped curve, and to these must have been attached a removable handle of bamboo or twisted fibres in the majority of cases. Today's omnipresent Japanese teapot has a four thousand year heritage.

Technical improvements had been effected by the end of Late Jōmon that were instrumental in changing the appearance of the pottery—at least temporarily in some areas. These transformations must have been due to firing in a partial enclosure at a temperature that was now somewhere between 600° and 700°C. The pottery is thinner, baked to the same colour throughout in shades of black, brown and grey; the clay is usually more pure; the surface sometimes burnished. Surface

Fig. 10 (9)

polishing to a metallic lustre is typical of the Goryo type in Kyūshū, and may also be seen in numerous Kamegaoka examples. Kyūshū, the Chūgoku and the Kansai resort to crude and rough surface marking before Jōmon pottery is supplanted by Yayoi, and the Kantō is not entirely free from it as well, but in the North the Kamegaoka types salvage lost prestige by putting on a handsome display of craftsmanship that is another plateau in the Neolithic art. The North had always exploited the decorative possibilities of cord-impressing.

Plate 14

Localized types like Akagawa are a little coarse when compared to the regularity of the impressions on the typical cylindrical

Fig. 10 (60, 63)

types, the standard types of the Early and beginning of Middle Jōmon. The North is not without its flairs and peculiarities:

Fig. 10 (64, 67)

Daigi potters were gifted with a keen sense of design; Ōyu craftsmen affixed long and ungainly spouts to many vessels; a Late Jōmon vase from present Hirosaki city, Aomori, bears in

Plate 16

flattened relief a human figure with arms dropping in right angles at the elbows, legs apart, feet absorbed into the horizontal bands of decoration. Northern potters by and large made their vessels smaller during the Kamegaoka period. They often pre-ferred vertical lines, and built the vessels up in two or three sections into silhouettes of much variety. Some jars are black with highly polished surfaces; others are painted red, parti-cularly if from Korekawa, and were probably intended to resemble lacquer from that site. All but the few that are almost entirely covered with diagonal cord-impression are decorated with slender sinuous patterns that somewhat resemble long bones, highly simplified birds or animals repeated systemati-cally. The designs themselves may be rather complex, especially when they do not need to conform to a narrow frieze of decora-tion, as on the underside of a bowl. There is every likelihood that these patterns are derived from bird and animal configura-tions on Chinese bronze mirrors and perhaps lacquer ware, as the former, at least, were already being imported by this time to satisfy demands of the Yayoi people. Recent dating of Yayoi pottery in the southern Tōhoku seems to suggest that the time element meets the requirement of this relationship. The last Kamegaoka change is one to *eau courante* which is in this area due to a reduction of the elements of the more complicated designs combined with the incorporation of influences, late in arriving, from Yayoi sources.

Fig. 10 (69, 71)

Plate 15

Hokkaidō shares with the Tōhoku the early shell-stamped, the cylindrical, the zone cord-impressed and the Kamegaoka types, but its own peculiar character may be seen in the Zenhoku and Kohoku types, and along the northern coast the Okhotsk Sea ware. Zenhoku is comprised of cord-impressed jars frequently horizontally incised, and vessels oval in section with small rim peaks and body ridges of clay. In later Kohoku pottery the influence of metal containers is quite apparent in the seams that simulate metal joints. Early Okhotsk Sea pottery is still occasionally cord-impressed, but it is also stamped with various small and graphic designs, and often decorated with many thin ribbons of clay applied horizontally. This pottery has a distinctive black, grey, or brownish grey colour. The discovery with Okhotsk Sea pottery of metal swords of Japanese manufacture datable to the eighth century is sufficient evidence to demonstrate that this culture lasts well into historical times in coastal zones.

CUSTOMS AND SYMBOLS

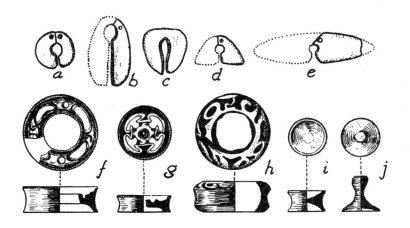

Fig. 11 *Ear-rings of the Jōmon period: a–e stone, f–j clay: (a, c) Kō, Ōsaka, (b) Chidorikubo, Tokyo, (d) Takagi, Nagano, (e) Yabase, Tottori, (f) Shimizu Park, Chiba, (g) uncertain, (h) Numazu, Miyagi, (i) Ikawatsu, Aichi, (j) Fukuda, Ibaragi*

The desire to adorn the body is already in evidence in Earliest Jōmon times when rings of small shells and horns of the wild boar were made into ear ornaments. For such purposes clay, stone and animals' teeth were also used, the clay ones becoming progressively larger and more elaborate until by the Angyo stage sizeable circular rings in pulley-shape were fashioned with considerable skill. Although there may have been instances in which these were suspended in the same way as balls of

Fig. 11f–h

stone and clay for dangling ear-rings were, they were also
inserted into the lobe, if one can judge by the information
imparted by late figurines. Smaller ones, some on the lines of ear-
plugs, were in current use from Middle Jōmon onwards. Flat
stone ornaments fitting on to the lobe were introduced by the
Moroiso people in the circular shape; brittle and prone to
break, these were often repaired by drilling holes and tying the
fractured parts together. Hair-pins and combs of bone decorated

Plate 20
Fig. 11j

Fig. 11a

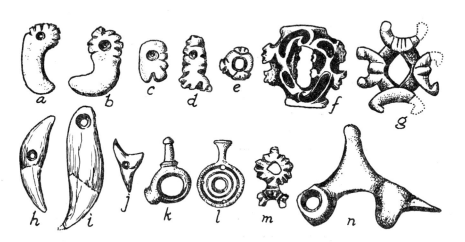

Fig. 12   Ornaments and amulets of the Jōmon period: (a) *Aso, Akita,* (b) *Hosogoe, Aomori,*
(c) *Sezawa, Miyagi,* (d) *Korekawa, Aomori,* (e, g, j, l, m) *Numazu, Miyagi,* (f) *Ichinohe, Akita,*
(h) *Shimpukuji, Saitama,* (i) *Todoroki, Kumamoto,* (k, n) *Tsugumo, Okayama*

the hair. Amulets, costume and body ornaments may be seen
in great variety, especially in later northern sites where they are
frequently coated with red paint. A claw or tooth, perforated
at one end, served as the earliest *magatama*, the later curved
jewel of imperial fame. However, towards the close of the
Jōmon period these were being cut out of stone in the North,
and had already assumed the comma shape they were to retain
permanently, and were occasionally notched around the head.

Fig. 12a, b

Some of the ornate carving of various objects distracts attention from what was probably the simple practical function of hold-ing sections of clothing together, like a buckle or hook. Shell bracelets are often found in quantity on the lower arms of skeletons; wearing these was more in custom in South Japan, but such shell-rings influenced the making of rings for ear ornaments in the Kantō area in that the clay ones are frequently thin and fragile.

With regard to body mutilation, the figurines suggest that tattooing was practised by Neolithic peoples, but one must be selective when attempting literal interpretations of the highly fanciful figures. On the other hand, at about the attainment of maturity, perhaps seventeen or eighteen in this case, in some tribes it was customary to perform a rite that involved the extraction of certain teeth, and possibly at the same time the filing down of others. Members of both sexes underwent this ritual, and there is a little indication that the teeth extracted differed with the sex. Canines and incisors of both jaws, but not always the same ones, had been removed in the case of 114 of the 121 skulls found by Kiyono in the Yoshigo shell-mound, Aichi. Later discoveries there by the Commission for the Protection of Cultural Properties showed that this was the case with eleven of twelve crania. Of the previous 121, only four had V-shaped notches filed in as many as four front teeth, and of these, two belonged to male skeletons, two to female. At Tsugumo, Okayama, almost all the skulls of eighty-three individuals showed teeth mutilation. This practice is of south-ern origin, and seems not to have made its way into Japan before Late Jōmon times, although the relatively meagre number of crania found before that time may be too few for proof. The practice eventually permeated North Honshū, and may be seen in Kamegaoka remains; later Yayoi people continued it.

Clay figurines were kept in many households and must have received special veneration from the adult female members of the population as symbols of fertility and protection during child-birth. One found at Nakayashiki, Kanagawa, had the bone of an infant baked into it, a pathetic sign that a mother was beseeching the deity of reproduction for further offspring. In a dwelling at Togaruishi small stones laid in a circle about 16 inches in diameter surrounded a figurine, and at Koshigo, also in Nagano, two were contained in a cist-like arrangement of stones. At Sugisawa, Yamagata, a Kamegaoka type of figure had been laid in a shallow depression; three stones were placed around its head and shoulders, and these were covered with a larger fourth stone. The head was directed towards the north. Although these instances have to do with a very small percentage of the more than a thousand figurines that have been discovered, nevertheless they are leads in determining the significance of the images in Jōmon society. Some of the later figurines have been painted red; many, like the plaques, have been rubbed smooth to the point of wearing off upper layers of decoration; now and again they have perforations in the stub-hands and ears, and were most likely suspended inside the house. Obviously these were objects of much attention, the *penates* of Jōmon times, possibly later evolving into the more modern Ainu goddess of the hearth. Dwelling H at Hiraide, which contained all the figurines found at that village, is not distinctive enough to imply that it need necessarily have been the residence of the local shaman, and the lack of consistency in style of figurines would preclude the likelihood that it was a workshop; rather it must have been a building set apart in this community for a specific purpose, probably something on the order of a parturition house, and its destruction by fire may have been intentional for the requirements of purification. Parturition houses are mentioned in the earliest Japanese literature.

The oldest known figurine is a small flattened one of Earliest Jōmon that came to light in the Hanawadai shell-mound,

Plate 20

Fig. 13a

Plate 18

Plate 17

Plate 21

Fig. 13b

Plate 22

Fig. 13c

Ibaragi. There are, however, so few others between that time and the Katsusaka period of Middle Jōmon that one is given the impression that they do not subscribe to a continuous development, but are revived under Katsusaka period stimuli. In the dynamic mountainous centre of this period, the chief interest is in rim-heads and animal faces. These are first seen in Moroiso and take the form of felines or rodents chiefly, although canine types also seem to exist, and the apparent effect of representing certain distinctive characteristics leads one to believe that they are totemistic in nature. Few Katsusaka figurines reach a recognizably human standard; animal-like ones were preferred, perhaps because of the deep respect and fear for the spirits that were believed to be represented by animals. A head and torso from Misaka (once called Kuro-koma), Yamanashi, is cat-like in some details and rabbit-like in others, but added together it is bizarre and sinister in appearance. It is too large to have been a rim piece for even the most mammoth of vessels.

The next major stage is one in which the figurines are un-questionably human, the shape is sometimes rectangular but always simple, and sex features are normally only slightly indicated. The counterpart to this type in North Japan is fre-qently just a torso. In the central mountains figures may have elongated proportions, be bell-shaped so that they are able to stand alone, and have hanging breasts. The one from Satohara, Gumma, has a heart-shaped concave face that is slightly tilted back, a wasp-waist and separated legs. The most striking change takes place towards the end of Late Jōmon, immediately after the Horinouchi period: pregnancy is symbolized by a much enlarged abdomen and emphasized breasts. These figures also have ridges of clay for eyebrows that are joined to the nose; the eyes are circles of clay, as is the mouth, stamped or cord-impressed perhaps to represent tattooing, and there is fre-quently a long jaw-ridge running from ear to ear.

Figurines of the late stages of the Neolithic are found in a few sites in Kyūshū, in several examples at Kashiwara in the Kansai, and in the Angyo types of the Kantō and among the numerous and picturesque ones of North Japan. The Angyo sculptures are short and squat with complex silhouette; the large heads are topped by peaks like spiral horns. The eyes, ears, and mouth are all discs of applied clay. The more southerly examples, in keeping with the climate perhaps, are undecorated

Plate 20

Fig. 13   Figurines of the Jōmon period: (a) Hanawadai shell-mound, Ibaragi, (b) Maruko, Nagano, 14¼″, (c) uncertain, (d) Tokomai, Aomori

and usually suggestive of nudity. The northern Kamegaoka images are hollow, and are often provided with flat 'feet' making them able to stand alone. These are wide-faced, broad-necked and -shouldered, heavily costumed in appearance; they may have piled-up clay on the head, oval eyes resembling snow-goggles, a necklace, nipples and cord-impressed costume that is rolled at the knees. Many years ago these eye formations were identified as snow-goggles made of stretched skin in a frame, but in North Honshū there is little need for such glasses,

Fig. 13d

although the thick costume would certainly be very serviceable; rather these eyes must have grown out of the concept that the eye is the direct line of communication with the soul. Realism and symbolism are obviously simultaneously rendered when a garment and nudity are both implied, and variations on sym⁄bolic and realistic emphases are to be expected.

Enlarged eyes do not appear on all the hollow and crowned types. Surface punching is a curious technique for ornamenta⁄tion, but raised shoulders, stump⁄arms and legs are always acceptable. One rather odd feature that stresses the mask⁄like character of many of the faces is that the head is snobbishly tilted back, thus sticking the nose up in the air and sometimes dropping the eyes a little, giving a simultaneous frontal and aerial picture of the face. Possibly this could have been derived from the practice of placing such figures in a low position, say on the ground, as undoubtedly most of these are made to stand of their own accord rather than be suspended, and also the late ones are often too large for normal carrying. The Kamegaoka figurines and plaques, like the decoration of the vessels, were widely distributed and copied; figurines have been found as far south as Shizuoka, and pottery decoration in the Kansai has some Kamegaoka details.

Current with these statuettes are simplified and flattened objects that are a cross between a figurine and a plaque. These are normally headless, legless, and have short curved stump⁄arms, and projections below the hips that are a stylized version of the rolled⁄up garment. Oval and rectangular plaques of clay or stone are to be found in many Late Jōmon sites of the Kantō and North Japan, and more rarely in other parts. They may have had roughly the same magical significance that the figurines had, but they are usually devoid of all female character⁄istics. Some have perforations for suspension. A much simpli⁄fied head and perhaps a symbolic backbone are the only features the makers considered to be relevant; backs are usually

Plate 19

Plate 23

Plate 24

Plate 25

ornamented with curvilinear and spiralled designs. In the latest ones even the facial suggestions are dispensed with, and decoration is dissolved into a multitude of parallel incisions.

The few clay masks that have been discovered vary considerably in size; the small ones, often with holes at the temples, make one think of masks for dolls or figurines, with body of wood or grass. The most impressive terra-cotta mask was found many years ago at Aso in Akita prefecture. Eye and mouth outlines are cord-marked, and non-realistic details are space-fillers in the best Kamegaoka tradition.

Plate 26

A few clay animals have turned up in Eastern, Central and Northern Japan; these are small, recognizable replicas of bears, monkeys, dogs, boars and tortoises. Interestingly enough, the rodent and feline character of the Middle Jōmon figurines has disappeared completely; the stylization that surrounded them with mystery is gone; these are little more than straightforward representations of frequently encountered animals. It is generally agreed by archaeologists, however, that they were made and used with religious intent, being symbolic of the spirits of these creatures.

The artifacts of the Middle Jōmon period are replete with symbols that connote fertility. Not until after this time do the figurines become quite specifically female, but large stone clubs of phallic form, stone phalli, standing pillars in dwellings and other objects, more disguised but similarly symbolic, attest to the emphasis placed on the magical powers of the male organ. It may be that in the Middle Jōmon a desire for greater permanence in the symbols resulted in the making of these in stone that had before that time been fashioned in soft materials, or it may have been due to the arrival of new ideas among the mountain-dwelling societies whose receptivity responded instinctively and expressed these ideas symbolically. It is, of course, even difficult to demonstrate that these symbols were engendered in the mountain regions, but one centre of production is on the west side where sophistication replaced realism, and it certainly does appear that their diffusion spread from the Tōsan both east and west and later into the Tōhoku.

Fig. 14c–h

The stone club-heads evolve through stages that at first look practical, then become graphic, and finally in North Honshū take a very decorative turn, and are sometimes painted red. Up to a foot in length, the shafts were highly polished, occasionally curved, and a few were tapered like a dagger. The last of these bear *eau courante* patterns similar to those on pottery. At

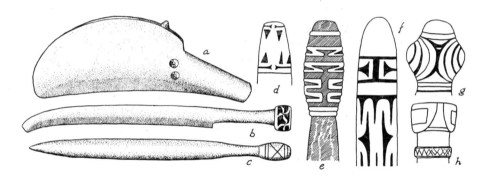

Fig. 14   *Polished and decorated objects of the Late Jōmon period: (a–c, e) Korekawa, Aomori, length of (a) about 15″, (d, f) Kukizaki, Ibaragi, (g) uncertain, (h) Bumma, Ibaragi.*

Kamegaoka, well preserved in the peat layer along with very late Jōmon pottery, was found a club of chlorite-schist whose head had been wrapped in strips of bark identified as a species of wisteria. It may never be known whether binding was customary, or whether it would have been done only for specific occasions, but one is reminded of the *inao*, the shaved willow stick that the Ainu mount to the east of a dwelling as an offering to the gods. No connection can be demonstrated, however, and the origins of the two may be widely separated in time and idea.

A standing stone club of large size was still in place in the north-west corner of a dwelling at Nishimura, Ōtsuka village, Yamanashi, when unearthed by archaeologists, and similar finds were made at Muramitakadan, Shizuoka, and Terayama, Kanagawa. While these instances are all in prefectures that are coastal, they are sufficiently remote from each other to lead one to believe that this arrangement must have been both customary and widespread. The largest stones undoubtedly stood as magical symbols of procreativity inside and possibly out, and

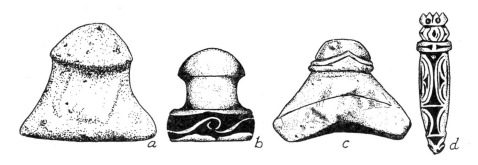

Fig. 15   Stone objects of the Jōmon period: (a) Muroran, Hokkaidō, 4½", (b) Ōzo, Ishikawa, 3½", (c) Mimmaya, Aomori, 4⅛", (d) Kita-nishirakawa, Gifu

the smaller later ones could be easily thrust into the ground, as they are single-headed and often pointed at the other end. The pattern of their discovery is not coherent; obviously not every house had one, and many communities seem to have had none, but this does not preclude the possibility that some households made them of wood or twisted fibres, or even as today, some families were less ardent believers in such symbols' powers.

Fig. 14c

The curved stone swords have no resemblance to known metal weapons (which could only be Yayoi in time), and must have grown out of some useful instrument in an evolution

Fig. 14b

that is now obscure. Rather late also are the finely ground and beautifully polished *seiryū-tō*, chiefly from northern sites. These resemble a cleaver, with blade on the concave side and a groove running down the opposite edge to a knob; conical holes appear just above the handle. It is generally assumed that these objects must have taken their shape under the influence of a metal type, and while traditionally they are referred to as 'Chinese blades'—probably so termed because of their obviously foreign character—their history cannot be satisfactorily traced.

Another group of objects whose symbolism is also unquestionably phallic is the so-called stone hats or crowns. At Hobi, Mikawa, one had been placed on the forehead of the dead at the time of burial, and certainly tradition has always associated these with head ornaments. Flat-based ones may have had their origins in a tool designed for cracking nuts or crushing and mashing grain, but by the addition of carved decoration they have been elevated to a symbolic status. The Ainu have a peculiar form of headgear that may be indirectly related to these stones. These and the so-called shoe-shaped objects frequently come to light in west coast sites. The illustrated one

from Ōzo, Ishikawa, on the Japan Sea side, has an oval-shaped base and was found in association with other stones of a magical nature: a club and a boomerang-shaped stone, as well as polished quadrangular axes, and a chipped axe of the type most typical of Middle Jōmon, but more likely with longer duration in this region. It goes without saying that the clay examples of these objects cannot possibly be put to hard use.

Fewer in number and also in clay and stone are small disguised and undisguised phalli. Later decorated ones are not unlike a reduced version of the late stone club, but carved from end to end.

Decorated antler ornaments are not unusual in northern sites, but rarely do they permit satisfactory identification of their function. The one from Miyatojima, Miyagi, is embellished on one side but entirely smooth on the other. Four of its holes in only two of its arms are complete perforations, two to an arm. Munro hesitatingly suggested a head ornament;[10] an often quoted theory claims it to be a waist decoration. On the other hand, it may have served as an ornamented spindle-whorl.

Plate 28

The shoe-shaped stone and the boomerang stone are west side types. One of the latter of sandstone from Tamuko, Taira village, Toyama, was found about 3 feet below the surface, but not with other Jōmon period objects, although Neolithic relics did come from the area. A groove runs the length of it on both sides, but only one side bears low relief patterns. Another one from Fukui has carved designs on both faces. These have been called stone knives although the inner concave edge is rounded and not bevelled like a blade. More to the point is the theory that it is a stamp for marking earth or clay and put to use in a ceremony of some sort. Speculation on the shoe-shaped stones often relates them to the grooved axes, which themselves eventually reached a stage removed from practicality. While this may be true, their shape is also surprisingly close to some of the stone phalli, and with those there is probably a closer connection. Such problematic objects may measure up to a foot in length, are well-worked and highly polished.

Plate 27

Plate 29

The methods of burial were not fully standardized, nor does difference in time seem to be a factor in the variation of procedures. About half were carried out in a flexed position in the majority of which heads were oriented towards the southeast; others may be extended, and pointed in all directions of the compass. Of the former, the great percentage were laid on their backs, legs drawn up, but some were deposited on one side fully flexed. Others lie face down, knees near the chest; or extended on the back, side or face. At the Yoshigo shell-mound one of the skeletons was surrounded by a black organic substance interpreted as a burial mat that must have enveloped the corpse, and two skeletons at Ubayama, and similarly at Tsugumo and Ataka, lay by burnt earth and charcoal remains made by a fire perhaps sacrificial in nature. The bones them-selves were unmarked by the fire. Traces of red ochre, parti-cularly on skulls and chest-bones, are to be seen on quite a number of skeletons primarily in North Japan and most fre-quently on children. This may mean that a secondary burial system was in practice by some groups. Other isolated occur-rences are of interest: at the Satohama shell-mound, Miyagi, an elderly man and child were buried in an embrace, both in flexed position, and at Yoshigo bones of an adult and child were found together in a clay jar. Flat circular stones were occasionally placed on the chest of the deceased for protection. The best example of this is at Kō, Ōsaka prefecture, where the skeleton of a fully flexed male adult lying on his back was weighted by a stone 6 inches in diameter, and large pieces of pottery were carefully deposited on either side of the head. Covering the body with stones and placing stones beside the head were also done.

More formal modes of interment include the surrounding by stones of the human remains, known from a number of sites in North Japan, and burial in a large jar. A total of thirty-nine jars for children were discovered at Yoshigo. In the 1951 work there, seven urns were uncovered, and of this number four contained the bones of children. This burial method was also used at Ōbora in Miyagi. The 1919 excavation of an entire infant's remains in a vessel at the head of an adult skeleton in the Tsugumo shell-mound, Okayama, has received due attention. All of these jar burials are late and most only slightly precede the Yayoi period, if at all, and could well be con-temporary with the incoming Yayoi custom of urn burials in North Kyūshū. The Yahagi shell-mound, Chiba, yielded a jar with a child's bones; this jar was thicker than the other pottery from the site and is Horinouchi in type of Late Jōmon.

Plate 2

The Yoshigo mound, again, revealed an interesting fact, though whether generally applicable is yet to be determined. The great concentration of burials both in jars and out was in the centre of the midden rather than on its edges, and seemed to reverse the generally accepted idea that cemeteries grew up on the outskirts of a mound. Also, by the Latest Jōmon period, cemeteries were compact, the graves close together. At Yoshigo the burials belong mostly to one period, but it is quite apparent that as often as not burials were accomplished and forgotten. There is a good example of this at Ubayama where the post-hole of a pit-dwelling barely missed a skull, and one pole actually penetrated a leg bone of the skeleton. The flexed burial directly over an extended one at Tsugumo would have to be explained in the same way.

The question of burials arises again in connection with the stone circles of North Japan. Recent efforts have been instrumental in bringing a number to light and elucidating facts on known circles. The count now stands at thirty or more in Tōhoku and Hokkaidō, and the reported destruction of many even during the lifetime of local residents must mean that this is only a fraction of the original number. The ones that can be dated by associated pottery correspond chiefly to Late Jōmon, the most ambitious period in circle construction, and others appear to fit in the Latest period. Many cannot be dated at all satisfactorily because of the absence of related finds, but on the basis of a general similarity it is believed that most either belong to the Neolithic period or represent a perpetuation of Jōmon ideas.

The great majority of these circles, especially in Hokkaidō, consist of stones that are rarely more than 3 feet in height standing in a circle, most often natural and uncut. The diameter of these circles varies considerably; some are more oval, but when so, the orientation too is variable. Komai's study has tended to show that some were cemeteries in which small stones were frequently laid in great quantities within the outline of menhirs. Human remains, however, have not been found, but this is not surprising considering the extreme humidity of the soil. Others provide no indications of their use or significance, but in a particular group that will be discussed below, there is much likelihood that early manifestations of stone and sun worship are represented.

This group includes those which have, among other things, the so-called sun-dial formations. This term is used because of its descriptive value. The ones at Ōyu in Akita are the finest and best preserved examples, but similar arrangements may be seen at Sodeno in the same prefecture, at Kabayama in Iwate, and in a few other places. The Ōyu circles are the largest, and also have a unique feature that inspires various interpretations. Two groups of concentric circles of stones approximately 80 yards from each other lie on the plain not far from the Ōyu River. Literally thousands of loose stones brought up from this river make up these circles; in the case of Nonakadō to the south, the outer circle measures roughly 135 feet in diameter, the inner circle 35; the other group, known as Manza, has a maximum diameter of around 150 feet, and the inner circle approximately 47. More often within the outlines of the outer circles may be seen stones arranged in a rectangular shape as though they mark the contours of a grave. Almost fifty of these were picked out by the excavators, and most of the scattered stones probably once contributed to outlining a great many more. A number were dug out and found to have pits below, and though it was not satisfactorily proved that they were used as graves, it may be assumed that they were. Also within the outlines of the circles stand a number of sun-dial arrangements that resemble the spokes and rim of a wheel, composed of long, river stones placed radially, with a tall central menhir. But most unusual are those at Nonakadō and Manza, in almost

Map 2

Plate 31

Plate 30

Map 2   Stone circles and other major sites in North Honshū

exactly the same relative position to the two concentric circles of stones, but placed apart between the two in a north-westerly direction, are separate sun-dials. The one of Nonakadō is the more striking, and slightly farther removed from the inner circle than the one at Manza. The similarity of the position of these two formations (only six compass degrees in difference) can hardly be accidental, and the significance is unquestion-ably suggestive of a sun worship ritual, not in the sun-dials themselves, but in the large concentric circles and fixed position of each isolated sun-dial.

The *Kojiki* and *Nihon Shoki*, the most ancient records of the Japanese people, put into writing in the eighth century, imply that veneration of the Sun Goddess is of extreme antiquity, and although the motivations behind this inference are largely partisan, it does seem likely that it was in practice before the Yamato people, around whom these stories are woven, organized themselves or entered the country. In fact, its origins probably date to the second millennium B.C. And again, the worship of spirits of stones, particularly stones of unusual and suggestive shape, is also a very ancient custom not to be disassociated from these Ōyu formations. One is reminded of the Izanagi and Izanami myth. These two gods were most responsible for the creation of the island country; they begat the Eight Islands, and propagated them with gods, though only after a first defective offspring. By way of inception, on an island near present-day Ōsaka, because of its central location, a Pillar of Heaven was set up; the wedding ritual included circling this pillar, done incorrectly the first time, but later amended so that the results were fruitful. One of the offspring of this pair was the Sun Goddess whose descendants landed in South Japan and eventually made their way to the Yamato Plain, the Ōsaka-Nara area today. Although the solar myth itself has little philosophical profundity to it, the ideas con-cerning its origins and subsequent history finally became sharp

Fig. 16   Excavated pit of dwelling at Yosukeone, Nagano

enough to reach a recorded stage by the eighth century, but the implications concerning its belief are for a long and very ancient tradition.

In addition, with regard to the link between stone worship and phallicism, standing stone clubs of Middle Jōmon times have already been mentioned. Of the same period are standing pillars in a group of houses at Yosukeone, Nagano. In the north-west corner of the pit-dwellings was built a stone platform on which stood a slender upright stone; arrayed on the platform and around it were such objects as stone clubs, clay figurines and broken pottery. Quite obviously the platforms and

Fig. 16

pillars mark the family altar or shrine which brings together concepts of stone worship and protection for the processes of and the benefits derived from procreation.

NEOLITHIC MAN

The earliest attempts to identify prehistoric man led to the inevitable conclusion that he must have been Ainu, since modern counterparts living in a stage little beyond that reached by primitive people occupy scattered villages in Hokkaidō. The Ainu today number approximately 14,000, but are rapidly losing their distinctive features due to marriages with Japanese, now more frequent that the development programme in Hokkaidō is under way, and in two or three generations may be largely unrecognizable as a separate race. Their unique customs are still retained, but in some parts at least are practised and exhibited chiefly for their value as tourist attractions: bear festivals, dances, thatch architecture, costumes, wood carving, and others. Where the tourist trade has reached an extreme, the Ainu curiosities receive the sightseers in a primitive hut surrounded by local art work and Japanese trade pieces; outside is a bear cage, the *inao* of willow shavings, and a row of animals' skulls on poles. The old Ainu and his family live in a modern house near by.

Plate 32

The Ainu are largely mesocephalic Caucasoids with Mongoloid traces that must have been mixed where their paths crossed those of the Japanese. Apparently they are of extreme antiquity, but attempts to pursue their line beyond three hundred years have been fruitless, for at that point the soil fails to yield any more physical remains that may be called definitely Ainu. This situation has speeded up the swing of the pendulum away from the early theory that Jōmon man was Ainu; in fact, partially due to nationalistic tendencies of the war period, the other extreme even was reached, though not seriously taken, that Jōmon man was Japanese. Nevertheless, one current theory is that the Ainu arrived quite late, perhaps pushing in from the north as the 'Japanese' moved up from the south. That would make their entry correspond in time to the Yayoi 'invasion'. Jōmon man has also been called proto-Ainu.

Studies of place-names have brought out that in North Honshū and Hokkaidō there are a great many that are un-questionably Ainu in origin; farther to the south a few may be derived from the Ainu occupation of certain areas, and others may have come about by borrowing. Historically the Ainu are known to have been entrenched in Tōhoku for many cen-turies and to have kept the Japanese armies at bay for long periods; the Tokugawa era records bear this out. There is much to commend the belief that the barbaric Emishi, known by various qualifying terms in early literature following the intro-duction of Buddhism, were actually the Ainu, as Kindaichi indicates, who were therefore living in large groups and are recorded as building forts in North Japan in the eighth century amongst other activities.[11] There are Emishi names in North Kyūshu and Chūgoku.

Jōmon man was not Ainu, however, by present-day Ainu standards, but it is unlikely that a prehistoric Ainu can be reconstructed. The white-skinned Ainu have more pure racial characteristics than do the Japanese, but they also have some mixed features, and if one were to subscribe to the proto-Ainu theory, among the ingredients of Jōmon men may well have been a group whose features later sharpened into the Ainu; they have had four or more millennia to accomplish this.

Before briefly analysing the position of Jōmon man in the evolution of physical types in Japan, it might be well to outline certain problems that have retarded satisfactory results. Most skeletons of Jōmon people were excavated in the third decade of this century at a time when Neolithic chronology was on very soft ground, and distinctions were perceived only between Jōmon and Yayoi. By judicious re-examination more accurate perspective has been drawn, but not without further controversy. The dating of the Kō skeletons is a case in point. Associated with this problem is the fact that there do not exist representative skeletons for all periods from all major areas of Japan, and, too, comparisons made between ancient remains and modern man in one region have found it difficult to take into account the shifting of the population during intervening centuries. Of the hundreds of skeletons belonging to the Jōmon period, complete ones are few, and the particularly enlightening statistics on stature are frequently missing from the tables.

The largest collections of human bones come from the shell-mounds of Ōta (69) in Hiroshima, Tsugumo (166) in Okayama, Yoshigo (332) and Kameyama (26) in Aichi, and the site of Kō (74) in Ōsaka prefecture. Other sites, most of them shell-mounds, have been the storehouses of skeletal material, but not in sufficient quantity to have received scrutiny and attention to qualify as types. Such finds include the shell-mounds of Todoroki, Ataka and Uki in western Kyūshū; Tsubue and Hashima in Okayama, Chūgoku; and the sites of Kamegaoka and Korekawa in Aomori, Tōhoku.

The oldest known prehistoric man was discovered in fair condition in the kitchen-midden of Hirasaka at Yokosuka; he may have lived while Inaridai pottery of Earliest Jōmon was in vogue. A mesocephalic adult male, he apparently stood 5 feet 5 inches, unusually tall for the primitive inhabitants of Japan. The Ōta and Kō people provide information on Early Jōmon residents, though only for the Chūgoku and Kansai. They are chiefly mesocephalic, and the latter is actually not far from the modern-day Japanese of this particular region, and formed what must have been the link between early man and the later population whose composition included heavy Korean and other superimposed elements. The Ōta crania are close to those of Yoshigo and Tsugumo but unlike modern Kansai Japanese. Kameyama skulls of Middle Jōmon are also mesocephalic, and also not far from the Yoshigo and Tsugumo types towards the end of the Jōmon period. Tsugumo man was of a stature that averaged slightly less than 5 feet $3\frac{1}{2}$ inches; his Yoshigo cousin was not quite as tall and nearer the Jōmon period average; these may be compared with today's Ainu who stands about 5 feet 4 inches, as against an average Japanese (if there is such a thing) approximately 5 feet 6 inches.

The evolution of the physical types is not without logic. Imamura and Ikeda see some relationship between modern Japanese in Kyūshū, Chūgoku and Kansai and those of proto-historic times, and further back, between protohistoric and prehistoric man. To these investigators, all things considered, Ōta man is the closest prehistoric individual to the modern Japanese; Tsugumo the farthest.[12]

Jōmon man was only thinly blended with Mongoloid features; this element later dominated under the large migration of Yayoi times, giving the Japanese people one common denominator within which there is much latitude. There are today still so many different types—the long-faced, the round-faced; northern and southern differences; country and city variations; dark-skinned varieties, light skinned kinds; some of these even bred consciously in recent centuries, but combina-tions of these characteristics in all areas—that one would hesitate to refer to the Japanese as a race; similarly, already prehistoric people showed gross distinctions, crossed before arriving and perpetuating the fusion trend with the types on the islands. Prehistoric residents were not of a single race either.

CHAPTER III
The Bronze-Iron Age

CHINESE RECORDS OF THE HAN DYNASTY refer, perhaps figuratively, to the country of more than a hundred kingdoms, but more specifically the later *Wei Chih* actually uses names. The exact locations may not be quite certain, but the most important regions are the following: Nu (Na), which must have been in the vicinity of modern Hakata; I-tu (Ito), an area that extended to Karatsu; Mo-lu (Matsura) was south of Karatsu; and Pu-mi (Fumi) near Iizuka. All of these are in North Kyūshū, the closest point of contact between Japan and the continent. The archaeology of this region in Yayoi and later times does little to delineate any areas of sovereignty, but the nature of the artifacts in general and the degree of specialization required for their production reflect a stratified Yayoi society in which ruling classes controlled the artisan metal-smiths and distribution of metal, pottery-making was largely commercialized, and rice production necessitated a farming class and perhaps others who were employed in its distribution. Iron always remained the workman's material; bronze became, shortly after the introduction of a new continental type, a metal used for ceremonial and authoritarian purposes with religious overtones.

The composition of this society, now of greater breadth and depth, included a nucleus of immigrants who probably dominated the upper ranks. Immigration was without controls except for the pressures resulting from people on the move and squatters' rights, and the relatively rapid and complete mongoloidization of South Japan speaks for arrivals in appreciable numbers. The new patterns of culture were soon absorbed in many old Jōmon areas, although several regions, notably Southeast Kyūshū and North Honshū, referred to in historical accounts as inhabited by primitive people, were strikingly late about adopting the imported habits. Also, an occasional Yayoi shell-mound is an indication that some areas, for a time at least, preferred the traditional method of food gathering, but were converting to new procedures by supplementing the diet with raising rice. Nishishiga, Aichi, exemplifies this admirably.

The slow beginnings of Yayoi in the early part of the third century B.C. do not separate its origins sharply from the Jōmon background, although its very existence is due to continental stimuli. In fact, the earliest Yayoi pottery, implements, burials and other features of this assemblage level are not easily distinguishable from the Jōmon culture, now worn thin by age. The power of Han expansion speeds up the momentum, however, and with the appearance of wheel-made pottery and locally made bronzes in Middle Yayoi there can be little question about the complete transformation of the western part of the country into the continental agrarian pattern. The movement of the pottery of this culture towards the Yamato Plain of the Kansai and farther into the Kantō coincides with the spreading acceptance of rice as the basic staple of the diet. Each century saw a step forward, perhaps slow in retrospect, from Kyūshū into the Chūgoku and then to the Kansai by around 200 B.C., as far as the southern Tōkai line of Aichi and Shizuoka in another hundred years, then into the Kantō by the beginning of the Christian era, and finally penetrating the middle Tōhoku by A.D. 100 or thereabouts. This momentum gained ground as the continental pressures mounted, and eventually carried the cultural centre away from Kyūshū to the Yamato Plain by the third century A.D., where it remained for more than a millennium and a half. Middle Yayoi spans the last century B.C. and first A.D., and is unmistakably the high point in continental contacts. Amongst the objects coming in on this tide were gifts sent to local rulers, some of which were noted in the annals and histories. Graves of the wealthy yield mirrors, coins, weapons, bracelets and beads, and attest to the monopolization of the riches. Much of this must have passed through the colony of Lo-lang in Korea where Chinese goods were plentiful and local copies had already set a pattern for what was to follow in Japan.

The restlessness and population movements centring around the rule of Wang Mang (A.D. 9–23) are indicated by objects that date to near that time. Coins of the Huo-ch'üan type minted in A.D. 14, though of course in use after this ruler's reign, and known in Manchuria and China proper, have been discovered in four places in Japan: Haranotsuji on Iki Island; Matsubara in Fukuoka, Kyūshū; Hakoishi-hama in Kyōto prefecture; and the important site of Uriwari, Ōsaka prefecture. The breadth of distribution signifies the depth in penetration of continental imports at this early date; and the associated objects, in the case of Matsubara a stone arrowhead and iron slag, and of Hakoishihama stone, bronze and iron arrowheads, record the contemporary use of both metals.

Fig. 17 Huo-ch'üan coin from Hakoishi, Kyōto

A gold signet, perhaps too good to be true because it suits the specifications too precisely, is claimed to have been found in 1784 on Shiga Island, Fukuoka. In the form of a truncated snake whose head is turned back and whose surface is orna-mented with punched marks, all in true Han Dynasty Chinese style, the stamp bears characters that may be translated '(from) Emperor of Han (to) King of Nu'. Since the *Book of Later Han* refers to a gift of this nature from Emperor Kuang Wu in A.D. 57, the Shigashima seal apparently meets the qualifica-tions. Nothing is really known of the circumstances of the find, but at least it symbolizes the current of the times.

Fig. 18 Gold signet from Shiga Island, Fukuoka. Length 1″

The largest group of early mirrors to reach Japan belongs to the 'TLV' type which attained its greatest popularity in the early part of the first century A.D. Few of these are dated, however, and after A.D. 125 Han Dynasty mirrors virtually ceased to be brought across. A revival of imports in the Three

Kingdoms and Six Dynasties period witnesses a renewal of the practice as attested to by the fact that amongst the several hundred Chinese mirrors unearthed in the tumuli of Japan, a number bear dates relating to either the Kingdom of Wei (A.D. 220–65) or the Kingdom of Wu (A.D. 222–80). Chinese mirrors and the copies in their turn also demonstrate

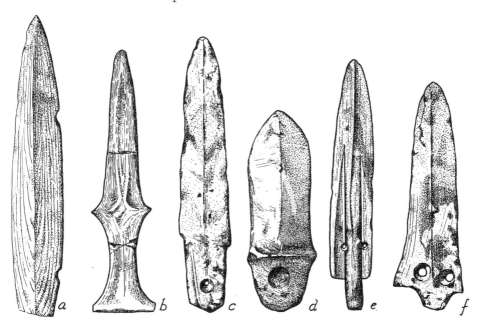

Fig. 19 Stone swords and daggers of the Yayoi period: (a) Munakata, Fukuoka, 14¾″, (b) Kawamiya, Fukuoka, (c) Yamada, Ōsaka, (d) uncertain, (e) Nishi-nakasuji, Kyōto, 8½″, (f) Itoda, Fukuoka, 7¾″

the depth of penetration of this Sinicizing culture at different stages; the Han Dynasty ones are limited almost entirely to the prefectures of Saga, Fukuoka and Nagasaki of North Kyūshū where the impact was first felt, and these mirrors are frequently disinterred in association with bronze weapons of distinctively Chinese manufacture. Not only were the mirrors symbolic of wealth and status, but they were also endowed with magical powers, a fact that has been much more clearly illustrated in Japan through careful excavations of tombs than it has in the mother country, China. The mirror in Japan had the additional significance of being the sun disc, eventually to connote imperial rank.

While this flood of imports was awakening the native population to the potential value of metal products, and was solidifying the position of an upper caste composed to a large extent of immigrants, the lack of raw materials became all the more apparent. In partial compensation stone reproductions were made of imported weapons. The copies are at times freely handled, but they probably carry on an idea that was Korean in origin, judging by the finds in the southern part of the peninsula. About ten sites in Kyūshū have yielded these objects that are sometimes classed as Eneolithic, but stone knives have appeared as far away as Sendai in Miyagi and Katamachi, Niigata prefecture. Doubt has been cast on the circumstances of such remote finds, but certain Tomb period stone knives are often difficult to distinguish from Yayoi knives, and also, an occasional object quite out of context exhibits a rare singularity of movement that one should be prepared for. The dagger with shaped handle is suspiciously Korean in origin; a number were found on Tsushima Island, and this is the type that is exceedingly close to the peninsular ones. The models of the bronze tanged spearhead and halberd, both with a pair of perforations, are realistic enough copies, but the former coming from Kyōto is a long way from its prototypes. By and large the stone daggers are not exact replicas of bronze weapons known to have been in existence, and there is therefore a possibility that some may be reproductions of iron types; particularly might this be the case for the simpler ones, and even more likely in the case of the knives with a single perforation. Most of these knives presumably precede the time of customary manufacture of bronze weapons in Japan.

Fig. 19b

Fig. 19e, f

Fig. 19c, d

Rice husks that left their imprints on Early Yayoi pottery provide the evidence needed to show that the Yayoi economy in its earliest stages had begun to assume a continental character. There is little to suggest that wild rice ever existed in Jōmon times, and at Itazuke in Fukuoka, a site that is transitional from Jōmon to Yayoi and expressly located to shed light on the changes that took place, there appears to be no rice in the Jōmon layers, but vestiges of grains are found in Yayoi strata. All the major Yayoi sites have remains of chaff or rice prints, usually carbonized, in jars or on bases: Uriwari, Nishishiga, Urigo, Toro, Karako, and a host of others; and extensive

Fig. 20   Stone rice reapers of the Yayoi period: (a) Fukuoka city, Fukuoka, (b) Ōkawa, Fukuoka, about 5″, (c) Iizuka city, Fukuoka, (d) Shinzawa, Nara

remains like Toro give a further picture of the plan of the community, its dwellings and storehouses, and relationship to the rice paddies, size of fields, and equipment used in carrying out the processes of farming and daily household living.

There seem to have been at least two varieties of early rice, though of only slight difference. One was in North Fukuoka, the other in the southern part of the same prefecture, but initially the grain was introduced from eastern China, from an area between the Yellow and Yangtze Rivers, to the rice of which it is most closely akin.

The ubiquitous woman's knife is further evidence of an agrarian society. These stone reapers were made in a number

Fig. 20

of sizes, even as large as a foot in length when they are usually without holes, but 6 inches and two holes is average. Roughly shaped and unfinished ones are fairly common. In Korea and Kyūshū a convex or straight blade was usually preferred, but in the Kansai one frequently finds concave-bladed knives, some-

Fig. 20d

times with three perforations. The holes, of course, held loose strings that could be secured around the hand. Iron knives of this sort were also employed, but only a few have been found.

Karako is near Kawahigashi village in Shiki county, Nara, and excavation started on this vast site in 1936 in conjunction with a public works project. It occupies one of the lowest points in the Yamato Plain, evidently a delta of the old Hatsuse River that flowed into the lakes near the centre of the valley. Preserved in the mud were the wooden farming implements,

Plate 36
Plate 40

containers, baskets, nets for suspension of pottery, and literally hundreds of clay vessels, often huddled in groups as if inten-tionally deposited together. Outlines of simple shaft wells were

Plate 37

uncovered, and hollowed-out tree trunks sunk into the ground for the same purpose were exposed. Karako is an Early to Middle Yayoi site.

Toro, near the coast to the south of Shizuoka city, was accidentally discovered when work for a factory to manufacture aeroplane propellers was started in 1943. Its excavation in 1947 has been the most elaborate carried out in Japan. Toro was a thriving community in the Middle and Late Yayoi periods, of

Plate 35

which eleven dwellings were exposed, and two raised store-houses. It may have been abandoned because of inundation, but it was this condition that preserved the wooden objects so well, and for centuries farmers have cultivated over the ancient fields with no knowledge of what lay below. The residences are to the north-west of the fields on ground which rises slightly and near woods that extend to more elevated land where trees were cut and hewn to suitable sizes for the construction and equip-ment needs. The houses are moated surface dwellings with stakes to shore up the bank; they are oval in shape, mostly oriented south towards the fields. A reconstructed dwelling, though not built over an ancient pit, has four massive uprights across which lie heavy beams, and to these are leaned dozens of slender poles; thatch is thickly overlaid to form the walls. Overhead is the additional roof member, still familiar today, that acts as both a ventilator and sun protector. The doorway

Plate 34

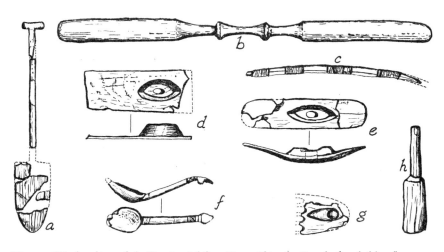

*Fig. 21   Wooden objects of the Yayoi period from Toro, Shizuoka. Length of spade (a) 40",
others to scale*

has its own small cover. Yayoi dwellings were customarily round or oblong, roughly 24 feet by 21 feet in size, and frequently provided with two free-standing posts at either end as supports for the ridge-pole. These supports were also used in the construction of storehouses, as in the one in fine relief on a bronze bell reputedly from Kagawa, Shikoku, and seen today in buildings at the Ise Shrine. These granaries were raised on eight piles about 5 feet high, reached by a log notched to form a ladder, and protected from rodents by rat-guards. Wooden

Fig. 3c

Plate 52
Plate 106

97

walls were covered by a thick thatch roof longer along the ridge than at the eaves. Two men climbing the ladder to a structure of this kind were incised on a sherd excavated at Karako.

The storehouses were in close proximity to the dwellings and only a short distance away from the rice fields. Thirty-three paddies were plotted at Toro, and were laid out regularly and

Plate 38

separated from each other by paths reinforced by pointed wooden slats 3 feet in length, in some places standing side by side. Irrigation controls were systematic and methodical, although undoubtedly not too difficult in such well chosen lowland. Nine of these Toro fields were 1,580 square yards, the average size, but one was as large as 2,765, another as small as 790.

Toro's yield in artifacts was primarily wooden objects that range from parts of dugout canoes to pieces of looms. Farming

Fig. 21d, e, g

tools include spades, rakes and hoes, all probably once tipped with iron if the local economy permitted it. Huge paddle-like wooden clogs for crossing the marshy fields are almost snow-

Fig. 21b

shoe size. The longest of the double-ended pestles for pounding rice outdoors measures 4 feet 10 inches. Wooden mortars are

Plate 52

large and identical in shape to that depicted on a bronze bell. Rice was cooked in a perforated steamer, and wooden house-

Fig. 22f, h

hold and kitchen utensils include mallets, spoons and ladles, fire-making sticks, and a variety of bowls and cups. A cross-section of these is illustrated, and reveal a versatile approach to shape, but consistent use of the *eau courante* pattern, a most

Fig. 22a, b

popular motif of the Middle Yayoi period. Cups may be footed, or built like stands, and fitted together in sections; one is almost completely solid, only very slightly hollowed at the

Fig. 22d

top, and though it may simply not have been finished, it is most likely a lamp-holder. The many pedestalled cups and stands of pottery and the known ones in wood, sometimes bearing painted designs, lead one to believe that lamp stands were much in demand.

These are rice-growing communities in low land, and one would expect rice cultivation to be restricted only to the most advantageous areas in its first centuries, yet apparently hill dwellers, either unable to move because of an active population already on suitable land or unwilling to relocate to adjust to the new economy, took over the practice of rice-raising. Quite a number of sites show that rice must have been cultivated under considerable odds, the best known perhaps being Tennōzan in Shirakawa city, Fukushima, well back from the coast and in low mountains. Much Yayoi pottery was found, and grains proved the consumption of rice in the area. Rice

Fig. 22   Wooden containers of the Yayoi period from Toro, Shizuoka. Height of (d) 5″, others to scale

must therefore also have become an item of trade for which bartering was hard in more remote spots, although one does not doubt that the residents of mountainous regions could always fall back on the almost inexhaustible resources of nuts, fruits and wild game.

The Yayoi people still found use for a large, rough, more or less rectangular stone implement, known in quantity in many sites, but they also ground and polished to a fine degree smaller axes in three main shapes, one of which is thin and hollowed out on one side, and another is notched. This last and a slender chisel with angled edge are primarily Middle Yayoi in time. Straight and curved chipped knives, awls and needles make up the remainder of the tool kit. Spinning and weaving was an advanced accomplishment by Toro times; circular discs of

Fig. 23e

Fig. 23a–d

stone for spindle whorls are not uncommon. Complete shuttles came to light at Toro, and from pieces an entire loom could be reconstructed.

A bow at Toro measured 1 foot 9 inches, and like Jōmon bows, consisted of thin strips of wood bound together by bark.

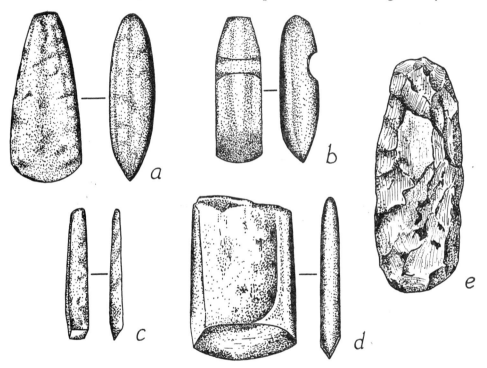

Fig. 23   Stone axes and chisel of the Yayoi period: (a) *Yajimamori-en, Fukuoka,* (b) *Yamamoto, Fukuoka,* (c) *uncertain,* (d) *Saikawa, Fukuoka,* (e) *Fukuoka city, Fukuoka. Length of* (e) *9″, others to scale*

Arrowheads were made of iron, bronze, bone or stone, but it is rarely that an iron one is discovered. Stone arrowheads fall into four classes determined by shape, the concave-based type being the most unusual and the tanged ones the most preferred. All were in current use. Animals and birds that were considered to be the fittest game for the hunter became favourite subjects in the graphic arts, and were scratched on pottery and cast on bronze bells, although in both cases not without some religious motivations behind the act. A panel on a bell portrays a hunter whose five trained dogs have trapped a boar—a completely

Plate 52

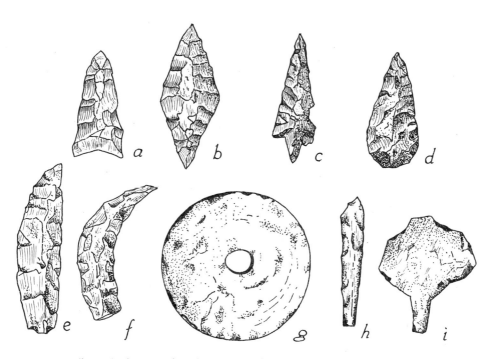

Fig. 24   Spindle weight, knives, awls and arrowheads of the Yayoi period: (a, c–f) Karako, Nara, (b) Sado Island, Niigata, (g) Iizuka city, Fukuoka, diam. 2", (h, i) Shinzawa, Nara

exhausted beast—and who is about to bring down his prey. On the same bell a hunter with arrow drawn stalks a deer, and two cranes are pictured on still another panel, calling to mind the fact that their bones are not uncommon in Yayoi sites. Two birds appear together again on a bell from Shizuoka prefecture,

Fig. 25b, c

a　　　　　　　　　　*b*　　　　　　　*c*

Fig. 25　Designs on bronze bells (a) Yao city, Ōsaka, (b, c) Nakagawa, Shizuoka

and deer also are rather often cast on bells. Unusually long-necked ones are incised on pottery fragments from Karako. Cow bones are, incidentally, known from Karako.

Fig. 27f, g, h

Although the gathering of shell-foods was not quite so routine, and the fewer numbers of shell-mounds of this period reflect the economic changes, fishing was conducted on an increasingly ambitious scale if one can judge by the larger size of the net sinkers made of both stone and clay. The Urigo shell-mound of Toyohashi city yielded many bone hooks, and shells and fish bones of both fresh-water and sea-water varieties. At Chitane on Sado Island parts of wooden oars and pre-

Fig. 25a

served sections of scoop nets came to light. Fish swimming in single file on a bell look like dolphins, and a boat that is only one of the many details on a bell in damaged condition from Fukui prefecture is sometimes interpreted as a fishing scene that would call for co-operative effort involving a number of craft.

Fig. 26　Boat cast in relief on a bronze bell from Imukai, Fukui

This particular illustration seems to depict one figure in the stern with an oar, and perhaps one other smaller head and torso behind him. A boat incised on a jar found at Karako has two men at the bow, one acting as both look-out and skipper, but

Plate 59

three unmanned oars are also shown. The artist may have felt that oars were all his drawing called for. Even these, as he worked from the left, were abbreviated progressively. Water birds elsewhere on the vessel remind one of the cormorant fishing of Gifu. The geometric and stick-figure style of the incised figures on the pottery and the cast figures of the bells have much in common stylistically.

Over and above remains of wild foods that have been identified by their vestiges in sites, specially cultivated edibles of this
period include peaches, musk melons, walnuts, chestnuts and
soya beans.

Weaving is not only attested to by the parts of looms found
amongst the Toro equipment, but actual cloth has been
discovered in burial jars. A mirror at Sugu had been wrapped

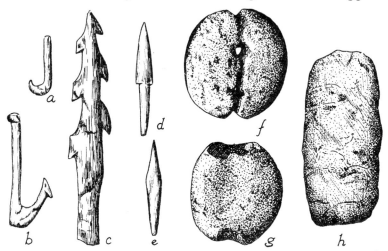

*Fig. 27   Stone and bone fishing equipment of the Yayoi period: (a, c) Kyūgo, Aichi,
(c) 3¼″, (b, d, e) Bishamon cave, Miura city, Kanagawa, (f, g) Kofuji, Fukuoka,
(h) Tateyashiki, Fukuoka, 2½″*

in a textile, and a fabric was found in a jar at Miai village,
Saga. In the Nishishiga shell-mound, Aichi, the base of a
pottery jar bore sharp imprints of what seemed to be hemp
cloth. Wild ramie fibre was probably used for the yarn of the
cloth that made impressions at Nozawa, Tochigi, and perhaps
at Nishishiga; both warp and weft are S-twisted, and varying
in ratio from 7 by 11 per centimetre at Nozawa to 10 by 24,
8 by 16, 7 by 14, and 7 by 13 in other imprints at Nishishiga.
The advances in textile production came about in the Middle

Yayoi period, and are believed to have been another contribution the continental emigrants made to living standards of Yayoi times, heaping more responsibilities on the woman of the house.

Such articles for daily use as farming implements, household utensils and weaving machines, not to mention the architectural paraphernalia that provided more comfort, were made possible only because of the availability and application of improved tools and carpentry techniques. Iron blades permitted the kind of finishing that many of these items required, and undoubtedly the larger communities deemed it essential to have the bare minimum number of tools on hand for communal use. Cedars were chosen in most cases for construction lumber and household containers; oaks were more sturdy and practical for the entrenching and cultivating implements. At Karako, cherry, mulberry and Zelkova wood satisfied the specifications for wooden bowls, cups and chalice-shaped stands. The present appearance of the objects is ample proof that surfaces were planed and finished, but painted designs on wooden stands are additional evidence that the craftsmen themselves believed that the surfaces were well enough worked to take painted decoration.

BURIAL METHODS

The Yayoi people buried their dead in a number of ways, but notably in cist graves and pottery jars. In a Yayoi kitchen-midden economy, the traditional Jōmon manner of interment was followed, but other methods include a simple hole in the ground covered with a stone if possible, or wood, often found in cemeteries accompanying jar burials, and rectangular or elongated shallow trenches sloping at both ends.

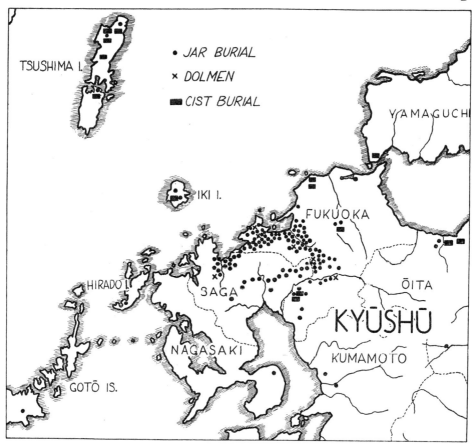

Map 3   Cist tomb and jar burial distributions in South-west Japan

Cist graves were introduced from Korea and quite likely represented an upper-class mode of burial. They are composed of thin slabs of stone sometimes very few in number, often quite neatly cut. These cist graves are rather unevenly scattered in the islands between Korea and Japan, in North Kyūshū and the tip of Honshū; they are most common on Tsushima Island, but surprisingly rare in the great concentration of jar

Map 3

Plate 39

burials of West Fukuoka. Since many cemeteries, like the one on Iki Island, have both cists and jars together, there is at least a period in which the two are contemporary. At Tennōzan along the Shimada River in South-east Yamaguchi prefecture, cists were discovered in a lower stratum and jar burials were higher—a situation that has clarified the relationship between the two burial methods. Another factor that speaks for a generally earlier date for the cists (without discounting the overlap in a very high percentage of cases) is that they most often contain no funerary accoutrements, apparently preceding the practice of placing personal possessions with the dead, but jar burials often do hold, or may have next to them, ornaments, mirrors, weapons or other belongings. Cists persisted longer in Tsushima, however, after that area lost its importance as a cross-road, and, too, cists there often contain iron, bronze and stone objects. It was only a few years ago that the reverse was believed—that jar burials came first and the cists were preliminary to and led into the later tumuli.

Cists are often lined up, more or less regularly, six or so in a group. An unusual one, Number 5, in the Doigahama cemetery, Yamaguchi, had been lengthened to receive a number of bodies totalling five male adults in all. Some of the dead were apparently buried outside the cists at this site, and though no articles were actually deposited with them, costume ornaments from the burial clothes were found.

The cists were Early to Middle Yayoi, but jar burials perpetuated themselves in a long tradition that started in Early Yayoi and did not cease in Kyūshū until about the time Buddhism was introduced in the sixth century A.D. But curiously enough, it was a custom that did not spread beyond Kyūshū, a phenomenon that can be explained only by saying that by the time it had developed sufficient impetus to move into the Inland Sea, the new tumulus mode of burial was coming out of the Kansai. Much grander and more impressive, this new practice captured the imagination of the population, and jar burials when used were reserved during the last two centuries of their duration chiefly for children.

Urns are known to have been employed in China since Neolithic times as sepulchres; they are found in Manchuria and at Lo-lang, Korea, but these in no way compare with the great number from Japan, and typologically show only slight resemblance. It may be that the introduction came directly from China and return influences filtered back into Korea. The two usual types are a double-jar arrangement, at times of the same, often of different sizes; and a single jar with stone or wooden lid. Urn fields may consist of thirty or more burials, averaging approximately ten a site, and instances of variations in pottery types in a single cemetery point to continuous and prolonged use of the grounds. Higher land than the dwelling area was sought for the graves and, being Japan, this was not hard to find in the vicinity. Obviously the lower land was more useful for the living, and the hillside could not be easily flooded. At Hie in Fukuoka city, the burials were to the north of the residences and separated by a ditch.

With the decline in popularity of the cist tombs, the aristocracy accepted the jar burial custom, although in retrospect it must have been a bitter pill, deflatingly ignominious after the pomp of the cist. Now the only way the archaeologist might even attempt to draw a line between perhaps an upper and middle class is by the size of the jars and the quantity and excellence of the objects found within or nearby.

The many Chinese imports from these graves bear out other evidence that the great majority of jar burials are Middle Yayoi and are representative of the time when these novelties were flooding South Japan. Then again, it was more proper to inter the foreign and exotic objects with the dead; the more native weapons and bells served other purposes and were frequently intentionally buried themselves, but for quite a different reason.

Chinese importations discovered in jar burials include glass beads; glass *pi* discs; iron axe-heads, halberds and daggers; bronze halberds, daggers and spears; bronze mirrors of the Han Dynasty; iron, bronze and glass bracelets. More native are the round, tubular and comma-shaped beads, the shell bracelets and various stone knives. When adding up the data it becomes

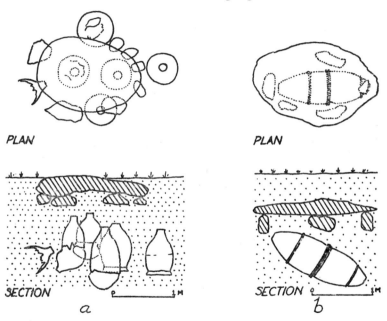

Fig. 28   Diagrams of jar burials protected by dolmens: (a) Hayamajiri, Saga, (b) Oda, Fukuoka

apparent that the deposit of such objects in jar burials corresponds with the middle two centuries of the Han Dynasty—the last century B.C. and the first A.D.

In dealing with the chronology of the double jars the trial and error experiences of those practising this method become quite vivid. The horizontal ones have suffered the most from the pressure of the earth, partly because as the earliest they are deeper, but also it was discovered that burial at an angle made them more prone to withstand the weight, so therefore in rough but accurate enough terms early ones are usually horizontal, those of the middle stages are slanted 30° or thereabouts, and the latest are laid at 45° or more.[13]

The earliest jars precede the introduction of the potter's wheel; the jars, however, are large enough for an adult, and usually two jars of about the same size were placed mouth to mouth and buried lengthwise. The arrival of the wheel permitted improvements in the potting and increases in size; it may have even been accompanied by a guild of potters and another of undertakers. Along with the wheel came a further custom from Korea—the dolmen-covered jar burial. Sugu, the leading type of the large double-jars of Middle Yayoi, is a cemetery site near Fukuoka city where over fifty jar burials have been recovered since 1899. The largest was uncovered in 1929 and had a total length of 6½ feet; it was oriented north and south, and rested at an angle of 30°. This particular one was not protected by overhead stones, but some were at Sugu, and slabs had been removed by farmers half a century ago. Sugu is also unique in that it is the only place where burial jars under protecting stones have yielded funerary objects.

Plate 41

These dolmens are composed of a single massive stone, sometimes granite, supported by a number of much smaller stones arranged more or less in a circle. As a group they acted as a marker and safeguard against possible later disturbance of the spot. In Korea such structures usually enclosed a cist, and the method must have been brought in while cist tombs were still being built in Japan, since there are two sites, Ishigasaki and Suwaike in Fukuoka and Saga respectively, where cist tombs are covered by dolmens. The method was then transferred to jar burials after its introduction. Quite typical would be one at Oda, Kitayori village, Fukuoka, where diagonally placed double-jars were lying a few inches below the stone slab, but

Fig. 28b

Fig. 28a unusual and not easily explained is the odd case of Dolmen 1 at Hayamajiri, Kagami village, Saga, under which five jars stood inverted, another nearby. This site was discovered in 1951 and excavated in the following year, revealing four megaliths. Both space-saving and presenting the smallest surface to the earth's pressure from above may have been behind the reasoning for inverting these jars. Interestingly enough, people in West Saga today are interred in jars, these being planted upright in order to conserve precious land.

Middle Yayoi pottery is of fine quality, the surface often brushed or well smoothed with a wooden tool, but by Late Yayoi the jars used for funerary purposes return to Early Yayoi coarseness, are not well baked, the bottoms almost pointed, and single jars only are preferred. The trend towards crudity may be due to the arrival of new burial methods to which the better artisans were attracted for their income, thus lowering the standards of the production of clay jars.

BRONZE EQUIPMENT

The bronze weapons furnish an interesting commentary on the way imported products were redesigned to suit local prefer-ences and tastes. These weapons fall into four main classes, and of these, three have both imported and native types, distinguish-able by size and quality of material. In the ones made on the Japanese islands less tin was used. One of these classes is a *Fig. 29a–c* double-edged sword, sometimes the size of a dagger, but always with slender blade and narrowed handle. Not many of these have been found, and the discoveries are limited to the prefectures of Fukuoka, Saga, and Nagasaki in Kyūshū, and Yamaguchi in lower Honshū. The shape that they take and the quality of casting and artistry prove their origins to have

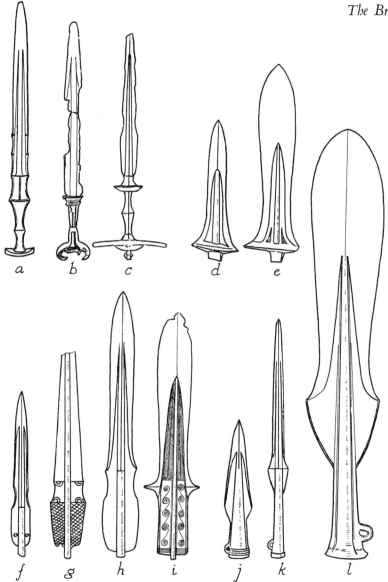

Fig. 29   Bronze weapons of the Yayoi period: (a) Mikumo, Fukuoka, (b) Kashiwazaki, Fukuoka, (c) Kōtsugu, Yamaguchi, (d) Yuhi, Saga, (e) Shimoitoda, Fukuoka, (f) Akiura, Okayama, (g) Yukasan, Okayama, (h) Futsukaichi, Fukuoka, (i) Yuka, Okayama, (j) Ka, Fukuoka, (k) Noma, Fukuoka, (l) Tsushima, Nagasaki. Length of (l) 29", others to scale

Fig. 29c

Fig. 29b

been continental; the illustrated example from Kōtsugu, Yamaguchi, is identical to one from South Manchuria; the Kashiwazaki and similar swords are like a China mainland type that is also known in Korea. Without question they belong to a very early stage of the introduction of bronze objects, the second to first centuries B.C., and a time before the Late Chou double-edged swords had disappeared from the scene in Han Dynasty China. The handle and pommel of the Kashiwazaki weapon is intricately worked into birds' heads and beaks, on an artistic level with the best of Han Dynasty craftsmanship.

Another class of weapon is best described as a *ko* halberd-blade of the sort that was intended to be hafted more or less at right angles to the handle with the benefit of perforations and a

Fig. 29d, e

short tang. The Chinese ones are usually smaller; the Japanese-made ones widen out through the blade. The other two classes are spearheads, one tanged, one socketed. The former is some-

Fig. 29f–i

times quite correctly referred to as a dagger, but obviously it is a cross between the two, becoming more and more spear-like in its Japanese evolution. Both of these weapon types are smaller in their earlier and continental form, longer with broadening blades in the case of the insular examples. The Sugu ones have a sharp edge running the length of the rib, and notches along

Plate 42

the tang for holding the handle on by friction. Daggers of this type are fairly frequently found in Korean sites. Another Sugu

Plate 44

find that is fluted longitudinally also has its Korean counter-part. These continental types of tanged and socketed spear-heads are often found together in Kyūshū sites. The socketed

Fig. 29j–l

variety begins as either short and sturdy or slender-bladed but always practical, and progresses until it bears a wide or huge, flat and much broadened blade in a shape that is quite un-usable functionally and equally impractical because of the light-ness and fragility of the material. The distinction between the continental examples and those produced on the islands thus is simple enough: the wide-bladed type of each species is local and, consequently, symbolic.

Weapons were the first bronze objects to enter Kyūshū, preceding the bulk of Han Dynasty mirrors by a century and a half, but whereas the flow of weapons dried up around A.D. 50, mirrors were arriving in ever greater numbers and Han mirrors kept coming well into the second century of the Christian era. Already by the latter years of the first century B.C. immigrant or native artisans were casting weapons in Japan, and these continued to be made till near the end of the second century A.D. Later, it was another wave of influence that changed the preferred type to the long single-edged sword of iron, the typical arm of the Tomb period, though undoubtedly the earliest of these were also brought in, this time certainly through the Korean peninsula and at about the same time that so many of the Three Kingdoms mirrors began to arrive. The weapons in jar burials are primarily Chinese in derivation. The halberd-blade of continental origin is occasionally found as far astray as Hiroshima in the Inland Sea and even beyond in Honshū, but its insular offspring rarely crossed the borders of Kyūshū and the western end of Honshū, apparently declining in popularity before the tide had moved farther into the Chūgoku.

Map 4

The tanged spearheads, or this dagger-spear, made the greatest headway, and the Japanese products have an Inland Sea concentration that is particularly striking in North-east Shikoku. Chinese originals of this type are actually quite rare, and these are the only insular weapons for which any attempt was made to add surface decoration; an occasional one will have geometric patterns cast on the flat surfaces near the butt end. Frequently these weapons are brought to light in groups of as many as ten or more, disassociated in every way from other objects, and usually buried on slopes or plateaus with impressive commanding views. Their role as symbolic and ceremonial pieces must have in some manner been connected with rituals that paid homage to or besought for greater favours the spirits that protected the plains and controlled their fertility, a practice of particular significance in the Inland Sea at this time.

Even more enigmatic are the circumstances of the finds and the meaning behind the three hundred or more socketed spear- heads of native manufacture. They also are found in isolated sites, often as many as sixteen in a hoard, lying horizontally and tightly overlapped. Four or five is the usual number. Seven in three stepped sizes of two, three and two were discovered in a specially excavated pit, perhaps boxed, all directed towards the south, on the edge of Usuki city, Ōita prefecture, in eastern Kyūshū. The smallest ones measured 2 feet $5\frac{1}{2}$ inches, the largest an inch longer. There are many other instances of this including three caches on Tsushima Island. On this island they are recovered from cist tombs, and in two cases in the vicinity of tombs they were placed crosswise as if for some kind of rite.

Even those believed to be Chinese may be of considerable length, and were an inspiration for the locally made colossi, but the latter far exceed the former in size, and are much out of the usual proportion between the continental and insular types. Partly because the trend is towards increased size—clearly demonstrated by the bronze bells—these are probably the latest of the bronze weapons in Japan, although the area of distri- bution would suggest exactly the opposite. In a rare case on Tsushima at Kubiru, which might shed light on the dating, the broad socketed spearhead was found in a cist with Late Yayoi, Haji and grey Korean pottery, a curious combination that might indicate a date for the spearheads of perhaps A.D. 100–300.

Shorter originals of this class frequently appear in Korea, longer ones only very rarely; the latter are also relatively scarce

Plate 43

Fig. 29j

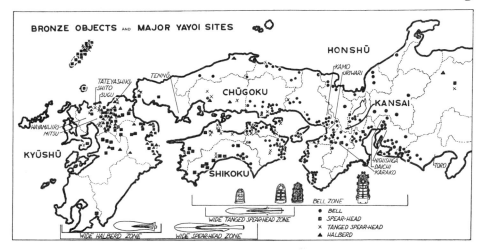

Map 4   Distribution of bronze objects in West Japan

in Japan, but are found from Nagasaki to the Inland Sea area. Wide-bladed ones have a Tsushima, North Kyūshū, and, interestingly enough, South-western Shikoku distribution. A number of stone moulds for casting the broad-bladed insular pieces have come to light in the Chikushi Plain of North Kyūshū, and the distribution also speaks in favour of the production centre being in Fukuoka and Saga. Moulds for this type and for the halberd-blade are the only kinds that have been found to date. In fact, even though there is much variety within obvious limits in the Japanese types, it seems most likely that there were only one or two production centres, and these probably in North Kyūshū. Whereas these socketed, wide spearheads reach well into the Inland Sea, the great number—sixty-eight—from Tsushima Island means they also survived longer in an area that lost its importance, as Tsushima did.

An interpretation of the religious and social conditions hinges on the bronze weapons and bells, although the expansion of the culture is more easily charted by developments in

Fig. 29k

Plate 45

115

the field of ceramics. Rice and pottery seem to have moved forward on a co-ordinated front, but the burial practices, manufacture of bronze weapons and casting of bronze bells hardly fall into readily recognized patterns of time and distribution.

In the old Japanese records which have much relevance to the Yayoi period since the social system was in the throes of sweeping changes, and rival areas and groups were seeking supremacy territorially and socially, the spear plays a major symbolic role in having divine power and at times signifying the presence of the god. The Sun Goddess herself was denoted by the Sun-spear (*hiboko*); shrines today sometimes contain a spear that had been dedicated to the shrine and which acts as a residential seat of the god. The dancer who performed before the cave where the Sun Goddess had hidden and had brought darkness on the land, did so brandishing a spear wreathed in Eulalia grass in a way that recalls the wrapped heads of the Neolithic stone clubs, and not without good reason. And in the propagation of Japan, Izanagi and Izanami stirred the brine with the 'heavenly jewelled spear' from whose tip drops fell to form an island, and the chain of reaction was initiated that eventually created the Eight Islands.

In a less abstract vein, however, two other passages are more positively applicable: one is dated A.D. 135 according to the *Nihon Shoki*, and states that when the Emperor Seimu appointed provincial rulers and village mayors 'all were granted shields and spears as emblems of authority'.[14] If one applies the 'adjusted chronology' to this passage a third century or Late Yayoi date in the Kansai is arrived at, and, even allowing a certain distortion in the late eighth-century writing, it indicates that such practices could well have had their origins during Yayoi times. Associated with this is a reference in the *Tsushima-kiji* which states that the shields and spears sent to the governors and chiefs were placed in stone chests and interred in the sacred hills of Tsutsu and Sago in order to ensure the protection of the frontiers. Thus, the divine presence and accompanying power that furnishes the safeguards for the countryside is nowhere more evident than in this idea, and must afford at least a partial explanation for these caches. If the Jōmon clubs stood along paths, as many of the isolated finds suggest, the new symbol of power, the bronze spear, was converted to this more elaborate use after its introduction to Japan, and endowed with additional authority.

One mirror type demonstrates that not everything new in metalware was Chinese or dependent on Chinese models. This is the mirror which bears a great profusion of fine parallel lines, mostly fitted into triangles tangential to each other. Two off-centre bridge-like projections customarily replace the dome-shaped knob of Chinese mirrors, and the rim is semicircular in section. The ancestry of this type is either Korean or Manchurian, and though many of these show a surprising mastery of the casting technique, the decoration belongs to areas that are peripheral to China where geometric designs along the order of saw-teeth and spirals were frequently appreciated.

Plate 47

The metal of the specimens carrying the most intricate decoration is thin and brittle, the colour black. This finesse of decoration, however, is not shared by all. Moulds of the coarser varieties have been discovered in Korea, and if the invention did not take place there, the development unquestionably did. One mirror was amongst a Korean assemblage that could pass as Japanese except for a single dagger: a polished notched axe, woman's knives, *ko* halberds of Chinese type, and this particular bronze dagger which has no exact counterpart in Japan. The information from this valuable context, to which may be added the evidence of a Shimonoseki city find on the western edge of Yamaguchi prefecture, where a mirror appeared with two foreign bronze tanged daggers, means a confirmation of Early Yayoi dating. The distribution in Japan is unexpected, however. In North Kyūshū and Yamaguchi they are grave-goods, but they also come to light as far east as Ōsaka and Nara prefectures, with no connecting links.

The bronze bells represent the insular Bronze Age in its most unique manifestation, and advanced stages in time and space. They also graphically illustrate the early artisans' inability to cast perfectly a complicated shape, the mastery of the technique with experience, and the full exercise of the craft in handsomely finished products. Various reasons are given for the theory that the bells are fully indigenous, shared by all archaeologists: first, in accord with the foregoing, the early bells do not show a technical standard commensurate with that reached in an area where long-experienced casters worked, i.e. North Kyūshū; secondly, the distribution, from the Inland Sea to the southern Tōkai, does not impinge on the zone where all Yayoi imports entered, and where most underwent their transformation to insular types; and thirdly, the likeness of the bells even in their earliest form is not near enough to Chinese or Korean examples. This last is open to argument, depending on the degree of similarity one seeks. If identical, the answer is negative, but if rather similar, there are Korean specimens that do suggest an incipient stage in the over-all bell development.

Nevertheless, in true Yayoi tradition, the earliest have a shape and appearance that at least borders on function, but later ones are progressively larger and further removed from any possibility of use as sounding instruments. Small ones start at less than 5 inches; the largest range to almost 4 feet. The circumstances of the discovery of the bells also implies a ceremonial use. The Fukuda bell (Fukugi village, Hiroshima) was associated with a halberd-blade and tanged dagger, both continental types, and proof of its early date. This is the only recorded instance of associated finds. It occurred in 1891, and

Plate 48

lesser ones along the sides. The saw-tooth motif is retained for the flanges. Thin and well cast, these are a rich green colour. Figurative designs have disappeared, and the panelling is a standardized feature. The late ones are concentrated in the Kansai, but examples reach back into Shikoku and up to the southern Tōkai, and of the approximately two hundred bells that have been found to date, a high percentage belongs to this last type.

The dearth of related objects makes the interpretation of their significance more difficult, but an analysis of the illustrations, even though these are limited chiefly to the middle types, should shed considerable light on their purpose. Most of the pictures have to do with the collection, cooking or preservation of food, whether wild or domesticated. Subjects are boars, deer, fish, birds, fishing boats, dances for agricultural festivals, rice pounding, a granary, jars for storage. Granted, the insects and small animals fit this pattern less obviously, but they may also have a symbolic significance in relation to the other subject-matter. The suggestion therefore is that the bells were cast as propitious tokens on behalf of the hunter, the fisher and the farmer, as an offering to the nature spirits for beneficial conditions to improve harvests, and were buried in a ritual act at a designated time at points overlooking the plains to secure the favour of the guardian deities. With all due respect to equally good ideas that undoubtedly have much merit, the theory elaborated by Buhot bears repeating. He suggests that the bells may have stood as protectors along the roads, perhaps covering phallic symbols of stone (which would not have been reported, since the moral persuasion of the Meiji era tried to ignore such practices while attempting to reduce its prevalence in Japan), thus the holes, first symbolized by the eyes and then punched through, might be intended for communication with the soul of the mould; the indentations at the foot would secure the bell to a wooden stand.[15] This idea then recalls early Champa where metal bells covered phalli in order to act as protectors of the fecundity of the land. The *eau courante* appropriately fits the role as a symbol of fertility. This thesis is not further developed to suggest what would have forced their removal from the racks. To this might be added, however, that recent finds have not borne out the possibility of association with phallic symbols, but then again, the thesis does not call for this association at the time of discovery.

THE POTTERY

The pottery of the Yayoi period is for the most part wheel-made and thus limited to far fewer shapes than Jōmon pottery, and also to far fewer methods of surface decoration. Moreover, the typology is cast in finer shades in spite of the fact that there were undoubtedly fewer pottery makers who worked in a time span

Fig. 30   Chart of Yayoi pottery

(1) Itazuke, Fukuoka–Itazuke type, (2) Itazuke, Fukuoka–Itazuke type, (3) Itazuke, Fukuoka–Itazuke type, (4) Tateyashiki, Fukuoka–Tateyashiki type, (5) Tateyashiki, Fukuoka–Tateyashiki type, (6) Sugu, Fukuoka–Sugu type, (7) Takahara, Kagoshima–Ōsumi type, (8) Itazuke, Fukuoka–Sugu II type, (9) Itazuke, Fukuoka–Sugu II type, (10) Isaza, Fukuoka–Isaza type, (11) Uranona, Kagoshima–Satsuma type, (12) Saishin, Fukuoka–Zassho-no-Kuma type, (13) Karako, Nara–Karako type, (14) Karako, Nara–Karako type, (15) Katayama, Ehime–Agata type, (16) Karako, Nara–Uriwari type, (17) Nishishiga, Nagoya–Nishishiga type, (18) Karako, Nara–Kuwazu II type, (19) Karako, Nara–Kuwazu II type, (20) Nishishiga, Nagoya, Aichi–Kaida-chō II type, (21) Karako, Nara–Shinzawa type, (22) Uriwari, Ōsaka–Shinzawa type, (23) Toro, Shizuoka–Toro type, (24) Mizuho, Nagoya, Aichi–Mizuho type, (25) Takakura, Nagoya, Aichi–Takakura type, (26) Uriwari, Ōsaka–Hozumi type, (27) Uriwari, Ōsaka–Hozumi type, (28) Hirasawa, Kanagawa–Suwada type, (29) Minami-miyama, Fukushima–Minami-oyama type, (30) Minami-miyama, Fukushima–Minami-oyama type, (31) Iseyama, Kanagawa–Miyanodai type, (32) Urashima, Kanagawa–Kugahara type, (33) Suwada, Chiba–Kugahara type, (34) Maeno-chō, Tokyo–Yayoi-chō type, (35) Shinohara-chō, Yokohama, Kanagawa–Yayoi-chō type, (36) Maeno-chō, Tokyo–Maeno-chō type, (37) Nagai, Kanagawa–Maeno-chō type.

Height of (24) 9½″, others to scale except (6) which is ⅛th actual size.

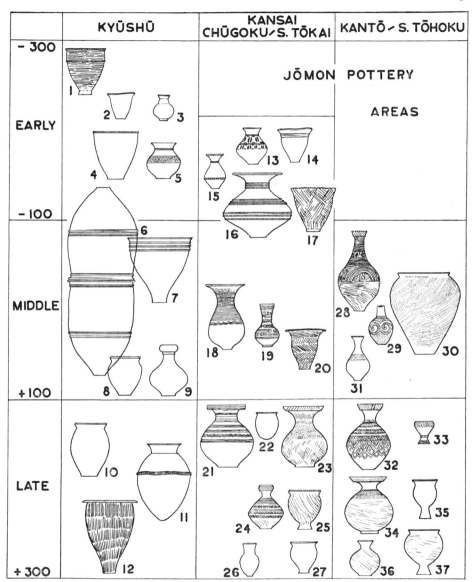

-300	KYŪSHŪ	KANSAI CHŪGOKU-S. TŌKAI	KANTŌ - S. TŌHOKU
EARLY		JŌMON POTTERY AREAS	
-100			
MIDDLE			
+100			
LATE			
+300			

Fig. 30   Chart of Yayoi pottery

only one fraction the length of that of the Jōmon period. The intricacies of the typology will not be possible here, as it was not with Jōmon pottery, and the chart condenses the more elaborate systems as well as omitting regions of lesser impor-tance but where Yayoi ceramics do appear, such as Shikoku, the Tōsan and Middle Tōhoku. Yayoi pottery is reddish in colour, and though variable, the paste is relatively pure. It is comparatively thin, fired under more controlled conditions than in Jōmon times, and the vase, jar, bowl and stand shapes have a consistently utilitarian appearance.

It is generally assumed that this pottery is continental in origin, but its beginnings are almost indistinguishable from the last stages of Jōmon pottery in North Kyūshū, and while con-tinental influences seem to be clear enough, actual importation of a new style comparable to the way metal was brought in is less certain. The wheel, doubtless introduced and probably from Korea, is not uniformly used until Middle Yayoi and at that time the continentalisms are sharpened. Whether imported or not, like all Yayoi artifacts, in the vigorous insular atmo-sphere its own nature developed rapidly, quite overshadowing any possible continental prototypes.

Yayoi pottery was first found at Mukogaoka shell-mound, Yayoi-chō, immediately by Tokyo University, and the term Yayoi came into general use about ten years later. The neck-less pot of that discovery is still preserved in the collection of the Department of Anthropology of the University. The first major discovery in Kyūshū occurred along the Onga River, Fukuoka, and the name 'Ongagawa' was affixed to the type there brought to light even though the remains had been so badly broken up by water movement that little more than sherds were recovered. Ongagawa has become the standard term for Early Yayoi in North Kyūshū; Middle Yayoi has been known as 'Sugu', after the cemetery site containing numerous burials; Takamitsuma has been used for Late Yayoi in the same area. Considering the fact that under these circumstances one is dealing with time spans of approximately two centuries, the terms are too broad and lack adequate definition; units of time of nearer seventy-five years in length are more practical when considering pottery.

Itazuke, the Jōmon-Yayoi site name, and Tateyashiki, the latter actually synonymous with the old Ongagawa, would replace the Ongagawa term in the Sugihara scheme.[16] By

Fig. 31   Red painted designs on pottery from Karako, Nara

shaving it very fine, the Itazuke type begins where Jōmon left off with much horizontal surface scraping, and a rim and shoulder band of clay, both notched, in direct continuation of the Yusu type, the last Jōmon in the region, admittedly virtually indistinguishable from it. There is certainly some question as to whether this is Jōmon or Yayoi, and if Jōmon, as it could quite reasonably be in an Early Yayoi site, the old Ongagawa type renamed is still the earliest. One would prefer to have a sharper distinction between the two before the Yayoi term is

Fig. 30 (1)

Fig. 30 (4, 5)

applied. Tateyashiki types may be plain or shell-imprinted, on which chevron-shaped shell-edge marks are most typical. The notched rim strip is retained, and the rim itself is thickened, a feature that extends well into the Inland Sea region. In the latter area there are strong local earmarks, but the vase shape has a rim, neck and body ridge, the last located at the vessel's widest point. Here it goes by the type-name 'Agata'. Some of

Fig. 30 (14)

these details enter the Kansai, and at Karako the jars have an out-turned mouth and thickened rim, and frequently triple lines separating the body from the neck. Karako has a red

Fig. 31
Plate 58

painted type in a variety of designs, the most characteristic resembling stylized leaves. This technique and subject-matter appear suddenly and vanish equally as fast, leaving few clues. It was a localized phenomenon, although over-all surface painting of Yayoi pottery is known from Kyūshū and the southern Tōkai, but a glance at representative designs, while dominated by stylized floral motifs, reveals a number of in-

Fig. 31e, f

stances of rectangular spirals and T-shaped designs reminiscent of the background decoration on much older Chinese bronzes. This may be, however, an incipient form of the *eau courante*, whose origin in Japan is still somewhat obscure. Many lids of vessels bear saw-teeth, radially placed leaves, circles and other painted designs, perhaps remotely influenced by Han Dynasty mirrors of the first century B.C.

Fig. 30 (16)

The Uriwari type is also represented at Karako; it bears horizontal neck and body ridges—an elaboration of Agata— placed on a body that is often very much widened, with flared

Fig. 30 (17)

orifice and narrow base. Nishishiga (Nagoya) vessels with notched rim were boldly scratched in a crude but distinctive way. This surface treatment is a feature carried over into Middle Yayoi. In fact, in numerous sites and types there may be seen both finely finished surfaces and coarse, roughly worked surfaces that in some cases, though undoubtedly not in all, suggest a distinction in use between storage and cooking equipment.

Yayoi pottery seems not to have reached the Kantō until approximately the first century B.C., the dividing line between Early and Middle Yayoi. Sugu completely dominates the Middle Yayoi of North Kyūshū in length of duration as in vessel size and quantity. Large jars were needed for burials, and these coffins of surprising standardization and quality could only have come out of workshops operating at least in a semi-commercialized system whose business dealt with funeral wares. The Sugu surfaces are undecorated, marked only by horizontal clay strips near the rim and where the wall starts to taper toward the base. The rims have a flattened out upper surface much like a T in cross-section, and are sometimes notched along the outer edge. Jars for funerary purposes may not have called for much decoration, but on the whole, the domestic vessels have even less; it is usually relegated to the rim. Later Sugu vases and smaller jars are frequently completely plain-surfaced but given a coat of red paint. Slips are quite commonly employed in Middle Yayoi.

South Kyūshū developed its own personality in individual-ized types, usually coarse, with only slight influence from North Kyūshū. The contacts ran east and west, not north and south in the island, a fact that is strikingly borne out by the extreme rarity of metal objects in South Kyūshū. Yayoi pottery, however, reached into Amami Ōshima of the Ryūkyū Islands, but is generally slight all through lower Kyūshū, an area where Jōmon sites in appreciable numbers point to extensive occupation in Neolithic times. Sugu, however, was influential enough to penetrate the south, and the Ōsumi type of Kagoshima falls within its sphere. In all likelihood the general abstinence from surface decoration, except for some notable examples, in this area may be traced to Sugu's influence. Combed patterns, and one of the latest types that sees the demise of Yayoi pottery not unlike the way it began, though this time with bold closely spaced incisions vertically arranged,

Plate 41

Fig. 30 (6)

Fig. 30 (7)

Fig. 30 (12)

Plate 54
Plate 57
Fig. 30 (18)

Fig. 30 (19)

Fig. 30 (29, 30)

Plate 53
Fig. 30 (21)

Plate 55

Fig. 30 (23)

Fig. 30 (32)

are clearly outside the general trend of plain surfaces. The wide and flat Sugu rim, and perhaps an elaborated way of treating the clay bands, even entered one of the most remote regions of Kyūshū—Miyazaki—possibly by the Late Yayoi period.

Combed designs are the primary form of decoration for Middle Yayoi of the Kansai where they are handled with considerable finesse. Often they are turned into the *eau courante* pattern, either combed or incised, a motif that is particularly prominent at Karako. Rims are of only slight significance at this site, but some kind of surface decoration is almost never overlooked. Combing is rare farther north; the old stronghold of cord-impression is first tangented and then invaded, and as Yayoi pottery moves more deeply into this territory it utilizes progressively more cord-marking. Zoned cord-impression may be a close copy of northern Jōmon patterns, as in the Minamioyama type, or used as over-all decoration.

Shinzawa is the Late Yayoi successor to the combed Kuwazu type of the Kansai. It may be plain or combed but the combing is looser, often in rather broad zigzags; a strikingly new feature is the much widened and overhanging rim. Variations of this rim remain with Yayoi pottery as it advances into the Kantō, to be cord-impressed in areas to the north of the Kansai. The Atsuta vessels from Nagoya city are usually quite globular in shape with narrow bases, and may have red paint added to the surface, sometimes along the zigzags.

Toro is the break in the cord-impression barrier, where its use on only a modest scale is to be expected. It is allied with surface scratching and in some instances with combing. Long scratches are not limited by any means to Late Yayoi, but are unquestionably a common feature of the second half of the Late stage, as are also simple plain, though often coarse, surfaces. A few pellets of clay appear as neck decoration at Toro; these ring the neck in the Kantō in the purest examples of the Kugahara type, where the necklace is combined with zoned zigzags that are cord-marked. The original Yayoi-chō vessel also has these pellets and shoulder cord-impressing. Its brother from Maeno-chō, Tokyo, illustrates how it would have looked had its upper part not been lost. It will be noticed that cup-like vessels with slightly everted lip tend to grow progressively taller bases until they eventually reach a point which is much like a pedestalled cup. In this respect the chart does not illustrate the extent to which the trend is carried. There is a multitude of stands for supports of round-bottomed vessels, and perhaps other purposes from many Yayoi sites. It is generally supposed that these stands in frequent instances were used in a ceremonial way.

Fig. 30 (34)

CUSTOMS AND RELIGIOUS PRACTICES

The bronzes of the Yayoi period represent symbols of temporal power with magical connotations, and however uncertain one may be of the exact application, they are still the furniture of religious practices. The substitution of bronze objects for the old stone and clay symbols took place as settled economic conditions brought a more self-reliant and outwardly materialistic attitude. A new definition of the powers of nature and revised expectations from such powers were based on the needs of an agrarian society. Undoubtedly rites and ceremonies having to do with agricultural seasons incorporated offerings and dedications, celebrations and dances. The burying of the weapons and bells is one facet of these rites. Possibly a counterpart are the clay figurines from a sand-hill at Miyuka Matsubara, Kofuji village, Fukuoka, found in somewhat similar circumstances. Eight rather shapeless images were discovered near the spot where a *huo-ch'üan* coin was located. Averaging $2\frac{1}{2}$ inches in height, these figures have holes punched for the

Fig. 32 Figurine of the Yayoi period from Kofuji, Fukuoka. Height about $2\frac{1}{2}''$

129

eyes and nose, and are widened at the base in order to permit them to stand alone. Their whimsical appearance is in strange contrast to the intense sobriety of the Jōmon period figurines and suggests a very different purpose. A little bowl associated with them is too small for any known normal use, and may have served in a ritual capacity, and together with the figures was probably intentionally buried.

A few but widely scattered discoveries of human-headed jars pose interesting problems. They appear to be products of areas where the Yayoi culture cut into entrenched Neolithic centres, resulting in the retention of traditional Jōmon features in a Yayoi context. The Ibaragi one came to light with three other jars in a way that also indicates deliberate interment, and the shape of the vessel is such that its most likely purpose would have been the storage of grain. The face may perhaps be a rare attempt to symbolize an agricultural deity. The eyes and mouth region are emphasized with red paint.

Teeth mutilation was still practised, but it died out towards the close of the period. One skull from Hirado Island belonging to Yayoi times is interesting in that it has a small hole in the crown, apparently made when the owner's head was pierced by a sharply pointed missile.

Plate 56

Plate 46

CHAPTER IV
The Protohistoric Period

THE DIVERSITY AND DEPTH of the protohistoric society, the intrigues of living and violence of dying brought on by the amours and other assorted occupational hazards, are all revealed on the level of the court and nobility class in the earliest Japanese classical literature, the two ancient records, *Kojiki* ('Records of Ancient Matters') and *Nihon Shoki* or *Nihongi* ('Chronicles of Japan'), as Aston may have correctly translated it. Both are the result of centuries of oral transmission, the former finally committed to writing in 712, the latter in A.D. 720. The reason for recording the old stories in permanent form was not only to put the stamp of continuity on the imperial line, sharpening it in historical perspective, and stressing the antiquity of its origins, but to state more positively the claims that certain clans had on the royal office and to emphasize their superiority through a successful combination of divine guidance and systematic conquest. To do this a great many sources were drawn upon and woven together into a complex fabric embodying outright mythology, borrowed Chinese and Korean accounts and legends, semihistorical adventures and factual events. Occasionally reaching epic proportions of literary inspiration, but on other levels equally mundane and often crude, the occurrences have much interest as thoroughly fascinating fables and fantasies evoking symbolic interpretation inextricably dovetailed with quite plausible accounts. The Chinese influences are almost invariably strong throughout; in fact, the *Nihon Shoki* is actually written in the Chinese language, and both were recorded in Chinese writing.

Only a very brief outline can be given here of the importance and content of these books. They serve a mutual purpose;

myths appear with only slight differences in the two, and much of the historical information, although more comprehensive in the *Nihon Shoki* usually, is largely similar. Their late date is frequently revealed by the terms in which the stories are written, when iron and bronze swords, mirrors and other objects were in customary use, but the greatest depths of antiquity are sought in order to initiate the formation of the island kingdom. Without fixed units of time sequences, the creation of the gods, then the islands and finally the peopling of the islands with gods took place in logical order. In the *Kojiki* the beginnings are unmistakably Chinese, associated with the *yang-yin* dualistic concept of the universe: chaos began to condense, but force and form were not yet manifest; nevertheless, Heaven and Earth parted and Three Deities brought about the commencement of creation, then the Active and Passive Essences developed and these two spirits became the ancestors of all living things. The Sun and Moon were next created. In the Plain of High Heaven the spirits begat five generations of Heavenly Deities, but succeeding gods were Earthly, and at the close of seven generations came Izanagi and Izanami, the 'Male-who-invites' and the 'Female-who-invites', the two divinities responsible for the birth of the Eight Islands.

These 'islands' are not all actually islands, but are in south Japan; the centre of the land was chosen, and it turned out to be an island called Onogoro, apparently one near Awaji. It therefore suggests that the sphere dominated by those who sponsored the writing of the records extended well toward the Kantō, if the concept can be taken fairly literally. On Onogoro the Pillar of Heaven was set up. More islands were created, and among the offspring of this pair was Amaterasu, the Sun Goddess, whose beauty was so stunning that she was sent up to heaven to take charge of its affairs. The Moon God and the Storm God, Susano-ō, followed, but the latter was unquestionably a disreputable character whose infamous outrages in defiling the hall when a festival celebration was in progress, flaying backward a piebald colt, breaking down the paths between rice fields, and other unsociable habits brought on his banishment from the society of gods. The islands in the meantime were drifting away from heaven's control, which may mean that restless tribes were trying to assert their independence, and the August Grandchild of Amaterasu was sent down to conquer the country for the virtuous gods. Emboldened and protected by three symbols—a jewel, a sword and a mirror—he landed in South-east Kyūshū and his descendant set out from there to find a more suitable location from which to administer his holdings. This man is Kamu-yamato-iharebiko, later known as Jimmu Tennō, Japan's first emperor, whose legendary date for staking his claim in the Yamato Plain is 660 B.C. The accounts state that he reigned for over a hundred years, during which time he grouped and regrouped his forces, travelled by water to North Kyūshū, traversed the Inland Sea, skirted the Kii Peninsula after tramping around the modern area of Ōsaka, hallowed a spot later to be famous as the Ise shrines, and planted the colours for the goddess at Kashiwara on the Yamato Plain.

Emperor Jimmu's clan thus reserved the right to call itself the supreme power; it had performed the chores of bringing hostile and unco-operative groups within the orbit of a central authority, but even the annals do not pretend that this was accomplished without disparaging reverses. Chinese accounts, too, referring to a country of over a hundred kingdoms (thirty of which were in emissarial touch with the continent) illustrate the over-simplification of the history and exaggerated claims for unity. One finds that actually three different legends are interwoven, their points of meeting rather vague and incoherent. The Kyūshū events appear to be the earliest, but another legend is spun around the Izumo region, now noted for its famous shrine, and a third is the more historical sequence of imperial activity and succession in the Yamato Plain. The Izumo people were very accomplished, as indicated by the references in the records to the effect that messengers were sent to that region to bring various artisans to the court. It is possible that they were predominantly Korean, whose craftsmanship later in image-making was an indispensable feature in the provision of icons for the Buddhist beliefs. Regardless of that, in some sort of reconciliation between the two threads, a compromise was worked out so that the Izumo people recognized the temporal sovereignty of the Yamato rulers in exchange for certain religious powers.

It is not easy to say why South-east Kyūshū was chosen as a point of departure for Jimmu Tennō unless a leader actually arose from a local tribe of that region and gathered his followers as he moved towards the Kansai. The reason for questioning this part of the story lies simply in the fact that South Kyūshū in Yayoi times, when this emperor would have lived if he was not a legendary figure, was quite poverty-stricken, entirely out of touch with the main currents. The tombs in this region are later in their beginnings than those of the Kansai, and reflect influences emanating from and not contributions to Yamato. The hostile Kumaso may have made a stay unwise and forced Jimmu to move on, had he landed there on his arrival from a foreign shore.

Undoubtedly as time went on the Yamato clans solidified their position and enlarged and extended their control. Some of the story is told in the major events of emperors' reigns after the time of Sūjin of the third century A.D. West Japan must have had its share of female rulers since the Chinese records refer to Japan as a country ruled by queens, and one of its outstanding sovereigns was partially subdued by this emperor. Expeditions against the Kumaso in South Kyūshū were undertaken by Emperor Keikō's forces, and the same commander, Keikō's son, also went north along the Tōkai where he fought the barbarians above modern Tokyo. Later, during the time of Chūai, further attempts were made to bring the Kumaso to their knees, the emperor himself dying in the attempt.

One of the high points of the semi-historical period is the story of Empress Jingō's assault on Silla in Korea. Although the attack of this state was supposed to have taken place in A.D. 200, it may actually be the expedition mentioned in Silla records as 346. The success of this campaign varies in the two nationalistic accounts, but the simple fact is that extremely close contacts were maintained with Korea after the time of the empress, and Japan actually dominated areas of South Korea, particularly the little kingdom of Mimana. Paikche and Silla, two much larger sovereignties, were also defeated, and warm relations were upheld with Paikche, the weaker of the two. Ultimately it was from Paikche on the far side of the peninsula that so much Buddhist culture was brought over.

Documentation does not begin with the introduction of Buddhism on this aspect of continental contacts between China and Japan as well as Korea and Japan, but after the third century (the third century illustrated by the number of Chinese mirrors in Japanese tombs) direct links with China became fewer and ties with Korea were tightened. The fourth, fifth and sixth centuries were periods in which entire groups migrated, taking up residence in Japan, and the advent of Buddhism is only a dramatized incident in the long and close association between the two regions. During the seventh century it was once again Chinese culture that became the supreme model, the history in Japan merely reflecting the fortunes of fluctuating power on the continent.

Reliability in dating in the ancient Japanese chronicles is not found before the fifth century A.D., as is indicated when they are cross-checked with Korean and Chinese annals, but from the early part of the century they became progressively more exact. By telescoping the centuries to about five hundred years, the excessively long reigns—one Chinese reference that the people of West Japan were a long-lived race notwithstanding—fall into an intelligible pattern. Suggested relative dates (with which full concurrence is not expected) are given in the appended List of Emperors; if a ruler's life span is noted in the books, it is included in this list, and thus one sees that both ages and reign-lengths grow more natural as the time of writing of the histories is approached.

The old chronicles make no pretence at describing society as it existed, but the social make-up shows through chiefly where the slaves, retainers, guild and corporation members, and petty nobles perform services required by the *élite* and imperial clique. Slaves were apparently rather few in number and must have been prisoners of war. On the serf level, or at least without freedom of movement and choice of occupation, were the workers who filled the ranks of the guilds. To a great extent the occupations were hereditary and their products were upper-class commodities. These guilds (*be*) covered a wide range of employment, and still today may have their vestiges as the last syllable in a family name. They were potters, clerks, fishermen, weavers, military personnel, soothsayers, actors, midwives, and almost anything else that can be named. As the society increased in complexity more and more of these were organized. The corporation (*tomo*) played much the same role as the guild, and both were usually associated with a clan in a way that provided each clan with all kinds of workmen to make it self-sufficient. The clan chief in this strongly patriarchal society owed his position to the hereditary system and swore allegiance to the head of the Imperial Clan, the emperor him-self; imperial rule was therefore through the headman of each clan. It goes without saying that many of the clans were closely related. The various ranks of nobility depended to a consider-able extent on the size of the clan and the territory within its power. Controls may have been loose under the feudal system, but those who joined late were not rewarded with plush fiefs. The sanctity of divine ancestry was zealously guarded; status was always of crowning importance.

THE COMMUNITIES

The ten thousand or more tombs of the protohistoric period hardly require a trained eye to pick them out of the landscape; the community site is a rare archaeological discovery. Most dwelling areas are identified by fragments of Haji pottery and iron amongst the debris. A few bronze objects and Sue and Haji pottery in shell-mounds attest to the fact that in some areas sea foods were still a staple item in the diet. Pit-, surface- and raised-dwellings were all in vogue; Hiraide, for instance, was a flourishing Haji period village, its forty-nine pit-houses almost all square in plan with four post-holes and the cooking stoves in stone or clay formations along one wall.

The clay house models (*haniwa*) from the mounds of large tombs are the most detailed source for the way farm and town dwellings, storehouses, imperial residences and religious struc-tures looked, and this source is so profuse when compared with the scarcity of information about Yayoi buildings that one wonders if the Yayoi period has not been unfairly judged. It should be added that other sources are also enlightening when it comes to reconstructing the habitations of protohistoric people: one bronze mirror from a tomb in Nara prefecture of the early fifth century illustrates four houses; rebuilt Shintō shrines have consciously and consistently attempted to retain their primitive style, and there are many references scattered through the ancient annals which have to do with parts of complete buildings that can be pieced together to visualize the continuing progress.

If the assumption that great architectural strides were made during the Tomb period is correct, the contacts with Korea and the wholesale importation of Korean workmen that did much to raise Japanese standards to the peninsular level may furnish the explanation. These craftsmen may have shown how to use planks in walls and roofs, and how to construct on an exactly regular plan, emphasizing the linearity with the use of rectangular windows evenly spaced. Other innovations seem to have included the use of mats for wall coverings; perhaps some sort of wall plastering, to judge from the appearance of the *haniwa*; gables reinforced by wide barge-boards; two-storeyed dwellings with full use of both levels; the entrance on the long and south side, of course continental in origin. It is true that these may have mostly come about by the passage of time, but they are known and frequently incorporated into buildings by the fifth century.

Fig. 33a–f

Fig. 33g–j

The house models fall into two main categories, one indicating preferences for new habits, the other regard for traditional, the former dominating in number: one is the upper-class town building, whether dwelling or storehouse, of sophisticated design, to a great extent of board and lath construction; the other is the rural building, also house or barn, built with posts and poles, uneven in appearance, mud-plastered, thatch-roofed, all reminiscent of Neolithic ideas but with more of the structural features visible.

Plate 89

The pit-dwelling was still used and sometimes in conjunction with other buildings, as suggested by the grouping of the houses on a famous mirror, although I would take this particular building on the mirror to be a great storage pit rather than the winter quarters of the estate owner. Frequently *haniwa* roofs only are discovered in a way that might imply that they represent the gabled section of a pit-dwelling model, or that the roof itself was already beginning to have special aesthetic significance. Some of these roofs are extremely fanciful, far more so than

Fig. 33 Haniwa *buildings:* (a) *Minamikami, Hyōgo,* (b) *Inariyama, Gumma, about 18", (c, e) Akabori, Gumma, (e) 18", (d) Tobiyama, Nara, 16", (f) Sakurai, Nara, (g) Minami–kanaya, Saitama, (h) Miyake, Nara, (i) Isesaki city, Gumma, (j) Shimomasuda, Miyagi*

Fig. 338

that on the structure from Minami-kanaya, Saitama, and make one wonder whether they could actually have been built or are just figments of the imagination. *Haniwa* buildings are distributed from South-east Kyūshū, through the Inland Sea, the Kansai and into the central mountains. The most famous group comes from the excavation of the Chausuyama tomb at Akabori, Gumma, where eight structures show much variety, but these removable roofs are chiefly from Gumma and Tochigi and belong to the middle centuries of the Tomb period.

One unusual *haniwa* from Kyūshū's traditional Kumaso area may be a clue to the problem of the *muro* in the literature, an underground dwelling in the early stages that later came to be used as an ice-house. It may have served as the standard reception hall, for Emperor Jimmu had a large one dug; he invited his enemies, who entered without suspecting a trap, and who were set upon and slaughtered after the feast. Pit-dwellings for the upper classes may have been furnished with more permanent superstructures. The core of this Miyazaki *haniwa* is obviously over a pit, wings with gabled roofs have been attached, and additional smaller houses in front and back resemble elaborate hip-gabled porches. A ramp should lead down under one of these. Its palatial character reminds one of a reference to the reign of Emperor Nintoku, an emperor whose beneficent attitude towards his people rated the deterioration of the palace of less importance than the prosperity of the land. The story, probably somewhat coloured, runs like this: at the Naniwa capital (Ōsaka), the emperor's palace of Takatsu was so neglected that 'the palace enclosure and buildings were not plastered, the gable rafters and ridge-poles, the posts and pillars were devoid of ornament; the covering of thatch was not evenly trimmed. This was that he might not delay the season of agricultural operations for the sake of his own personal caprices.'[17] Forced labour was temporarily abolished; the palace fell to ruin, but three years later the countryside was

Plate 103

flourishing and by popular demand a new palace was built. It is not clear how long it took, but '. . . the people, without superintendence, supporting the aged and leading by the hand the young, transported timber, carried baskets (of earth) on their backs, and worked their hardest without distinction of night or day, vying with one another in the construction. In this manner, ere long the palace buildings were every one completed.'[18] Despite the fact that there is something about Nintoku's professed altruism that makes one think the story may have been lifted from a Chinese history book, it may be possible to use some of the statements cautiously. I would apply them to the conscripted unskilled labour required for large-scale earth-moving if pits were dug, and the construction of palace buildings in the plural. Perhaps this *haniwa* illustrates what the palatial types may have been, or, if nothing else, the reception hall associated with the imperial palace, with an entrance and three strategically located guard-houses.

The surface-dwellings of the wealthy were normally single-storeyed, often with hipped-gable roof, or perhaps as frequently gabled with overhanging barge-boards through which the ridge-pole was inserted, and two purlins provided extra support. Only the *haniwa* seem to bespeak the two-storeyed residence in either hipped-gable style or gable roof with broken lines, the latter the preview to the typical Buddhist treatment of a temple roof. One might consider the tall buildings as equipped with an additional storey merely for burial in the ground—comparable to the tubes that hold up the human figures and animals—but the houses mainly have low vertical lines and stood on the ground rather than in, and do not seem to have needed the additional projection for vertical stability. In a single case, perforations in the lower level of one building resemble the holes in the cylinders of human and animal figures, showing that the house was to be partially pressed into the ground.

Fig. 33e

Fig. 33c

Plate 89

The tall, slender and more southern-looking structure on stilts, already in use by the first century A.D., the date of the bell, has given way to a more sturdy, native type of storehouse, although as a type it was either unpopular with *haniwa* makers or impractical for these sculptors to reproduce literally. The mirror, once again, pictures two raised-floor buildings of different roof types. One has the splayed gable of the Kagawa bronze bell and V-shaped projections at the corners; the other is a more substantial structure whose ladder to a balconied floor is graced with railings, probably an indication that it is a residence of a special nature. It may have the lack of space as an excuse for being the only building without birds on its roof, but it will be noticed that this particular structure has a number of peculiar objects in association with it. Natural rendering makes the trees between the buildings readily recognizable. The projection that is tilted to the left must be a parasol-like covering which acts as a sunshade for a kind of patio. Like the trees, it is disposed radially from the centre of the mirror. The space-filling geometric patterns to the right and left are the best preserved on that part of the mirror, and are borrowed from Chinese mirror patterns, but perhaps they still may have been used to mark the presence of rice fields in the immediate vicinity of the storehouses and dwellings.

The fact is that the chief early shrine types utilized the raised structure, and there seems to be a reference to the type as the palace of Jimmu Tennō while he was still in Kyūshū, if I understand it correctly. The *Nihon Shoki* says, 'They (local nobles) built a palace raised on one pillar. . . .'[19] That these structures for a considerable period were quite temporary is obvious enough, since the emperor was constantly on the march, yet a slightly later remark having to do with a three-year stay in the land of Kibi (Okayama in the Inland Sea) specifies his residence as a 'temporary palace'. In these unsettled circumstances a traditional complex of buildings would be a slow development. The mention also made in ancient literature that Emperor Suinin rebuilt the Izumo Shrine as a copy of his palace might be taken to indicate that royal residences were structures built on raised platforms. The raised floor was literally and symbolically a unique lordly position. Here, too, other distinguishing features were supposedly the sole right of the supreme rulers. In an unrelated story and thus told for its propaganda value, Emperor Yūriaku became enraged when he saw that the house of the Great Departmental Lord of Shiki carried *katsuogi* on its roof in imitation of the imperial palace, these being the cigar-shaped logs that lie as weights across the ridge-pole. The emperor dispatched his men to burn the house to the ground, but was finally dissuaded from destroying it when the Great Departmental Lord—referred to by Yūriaku, and also by himself as a slave—admitted in fear that he had 'built overmuch',[20] and made an august offering of a white dog. These *katsuogi* and *chigi*, the extensions of the gable lines, retain their special significance in Shintō shrines, where in a handful of cases the purity of the ancient forms are pretentiously retained, and the claims for divinity on the part of the imperial house lend much logic for identity between religious and palace architecture.

IRON

Of mounting importance in the activities of an increasingly intricate society was that utilitarian material, iron. Its real and immeasurable value in the performance of the menial tasks that formed a solid base to the economy is overlooked in the literature where iron swords, iron shields, iron targets and others are almost always spoken of in terms of weapons and gifts. It has not yet been determined to what extent Yayoi iron was imported or locally wrought; it may have been both, but by the Middle Yayoi period the Kantō was already in posses⁄sion of it, for pottery of that time has been discovered with iron axes at Akasaka, Miura city, Kanagawa. This may be taken to indicate that iron had been diffused into regions later occupied by the states of the Tomb period. The tombs have been the protectors of what little iron has been found, and the tombs are naturally repositories of upper⁄class equipment of practical and symbolic value, yet interestingly enough, an occasional farm implement, undoubtedly a hall⁄mark of rice⁄land ownership, turns up in one. Few changes were called for and few had been made since Yayoi times; the rakes were three⁄ or four⁄pronged, the wrap⁄around⁄handle axe head is new but widespread, the saw blades were short and required a lot of motion. Other iron items of daily use include scissors, sickles, fish⁄hooks, harpoons and a variety of arrowheads.

Fig. 34

Where the shapeless fragments leave too much to the ima⁄gination, frequently stone copies of iron, bronze and wooden utensils from tombs fill the gaps in information. Usually in an attractive green steatite and well finished, often painted red, these little stone replicas are a phenomenon of the Early Tomb period, and are particularly prevalent in the Kansai, Kantō and mountains west of the plain, in areas where iron was plenti⁄ful, although in this connection it should be pointed out that bronze was practically unknown in the Kantō. Since these replicas are sometimes found in great abundance in tombs, and are the dominant artifact, it may be presumed that they repre⁄sent a temporary local inability to acquire the necessary actual articles, or even the rather novel, however temporary, idea of leaving the originals to the living and sending the copies along with the dead. Of the great variety of these, only a small number are illustrated, some more recognizably ceremonial than others. Reproductions of wooden implements whose manufacture must have become thoroughly standardized if not virtually

Fig. 34d, b

mass⁄produced, like the rice pestles and walking clogs, for

which a stone copy would require more time, skill and even finer selection of material than the original, are a paradox not easily explained.

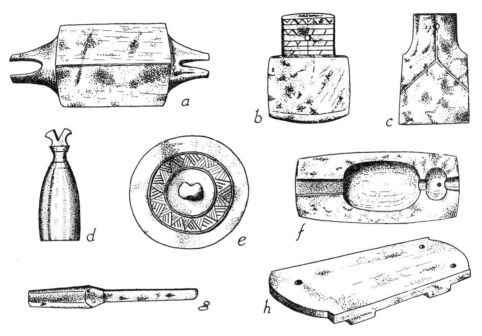

Fig. 34   Stone replicas of tools and utensils from tombs: (a) spindle, Minamitachibana, Gumma, (b) axe, Sakai, Ōsaka, (c) axe, Samida, Nara, 1¾", (d) pestle, Akasaka, Gifu, 3½", (e) mirror, provenance uncertain, (f) vat, Tamagawa, Tokyo, (g) chisel, Samida, Nara, (h) clogs, Ōharano, Kyōto

THE TOMBS

The dearth of dwelling sites in the Tomb period makes the tumuli assume even greater significance in protohistoric archaeology. Ostentatious as the gulf may have been between the aristocracy and the serfs, the wealth of sites, the richness of the deposits, the impressions of control and co-ordination of human effort, the unquestionable pride in achievement—at least on upper levels of society—leave one in awe of the grandeur of the accomplishments. It puts in the shade the underlying reality of social conditions that permitted the creation of mausolea of such magnitude.

A site for the Early tombs was logically enough chosen on the slope of a hill behind the valuable lowlands, but in an exalted position that dominated the countryside, and while individual preferences and topographical considerations are manifold, the colossal tombs of the Middle period are out on the plains, mimicking miniature mountains in themselves, and visible for many miles. The Late tombs may be either on plains or hills, perhaps partially because first-come-first-served land was running out. The mounded grave is more than likely a Korean idea, imported directly to the centre of the Yamato culture where the necessary power existed to see it put into practice, in an effort to match and eventually outdo continental lavishness. This happened at the end of the third century or beginning of the fourth in the Kansai. Within a hundred years the idea was appropriated by local rulers and lesser chieftains to the west through the Inland Sea to Kyūshū, and east into the Kantō and beyond. The fifth century is the period of the most gigantic—including those of the Emperors Nintoku and Richū, quite credibly traditionally correct in identification— yet it is also a period of surprising contrasts, for the reputed tomb of Yūriaku is exceedingly small and trivial by contrast— in spite of the fact that his twenty years in office would have been quite ample to furnish himself with a substantial mausoleum. The fifth century constitutes the Middle Tomb period, and the sixth and seventh, even beyond the introduction of Buddhism, are its Late stages.

Map 5

The concentrations of the tombs demarcate the centres of population in protohistoric times; most of these are to be expected on the basis of previous performance or frequent

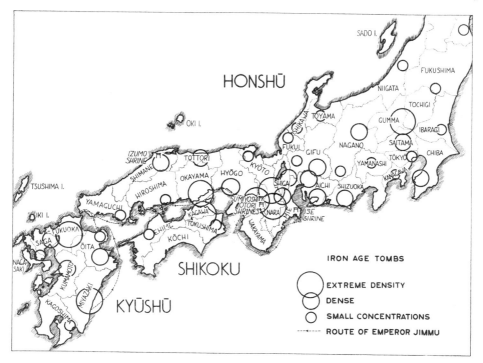

Map 5   Concentrations of Iron Age tombs

references to the regions in the literature, so that of the five major concentrations, three—North Kyūshū, the constriction of the Inland Sea, and the Ōsaka-Kyōto-Nara area—are the pausing and halting points of the march to the Kansai. But for all the maligning the south-east part of Kyūshū gets— fashionable to the *Nihon Shoki* writers because of the difficulty in subduing the barbarians—it must have been the fastness of an appreciable tribal group who died violently or naturally in sufficient numbers to strew the Sadowara Plain with tombs. This region is largely protected from the body of Kyūshū by mountains, and was accordingly chiefly accessible by sea; thus Jimmu Tennō's movement by boat. At the north end, an area that was densely inhabited even in Jōmon times, is upland Eastern Gumma, directly north of the Kantō Plain, and adjacent to the Saitama tomb groups that graduate into the foot-hills. Other concentrations in greater or smaller numbers may be referred to on the map. The important Izumo zone, the locality of the shrine, has its share; some Jōmon areas are revived, some Yayoi regions continue as centres, but other Yayoi areas, such as Kōchi in Shikoku, are virtually by-passed. It should be pointed out that the map marks concentrations only and does not show the scattered tombs which cannot be thus indicated. Tsushima and Iki, for instance, between Korea and Japan, have their fair measure, but if anything gives a picture of the Japanese landscape as the Chinese annalists saw it—a country of more than a hundred kingdoms—the circles of tomb concentrations come as close as reason permits.

Names themselves speak for individual tombs and their concentrations: Senzuka (Thousand tombs), Hyakuzuka (Hundred tombs); Tsukahara (Field of tombs), and the suffix *tsuka* to a mountain name, as well as Ōtsuka (Large or King's tomb), show how they have become geographical landmarks and an integral part of the landscape. Legends have grown up around many, and a widespread belief that misfortune will befall anyone who digs into a large one has been a super-stition that archaeologists could wish had been taken more seriously. A number bear names of Shintō or Buddhist gods, some with shrines on top or Buddhist images or altars within. Governmental controls to prevent vandalism have been as stringent as possible, and early twentieth-century practices to rebuild the prestige of the emperors were able, as a part of the psychology, to cast a spell of veneration around at least certain tombs, that gave them much social protection. Destruction took place in the Nara period, however, reaching such a scandalous point that pilfering was forbidden by govern-mental decree; particularly popular was the use of available slabs for stelae. Incidental looting has not been fully controlled, but the next great period of destruction has been post-war, when the building of roads and other kinds of construction, as well as the simple problem of a cramped population needing more and more land, has destroyed some and put new dents in many; this has been coupled of course with the lessening of their hallowed character. Small tombs are always being excavated, and it might be noted that archaeologists have had permission to excavate some large ones previously untouched, and have either replaced the objects they discovered after proper recording or kept them out and restored the tombs to their original appearance.

A number of different shapes developed as the period wore on. Round ones were always in use, of all sizes and proportions, sometimes terraced, with or without moat, and in rare cases with a miniature square projection on one side. Occasionally two circular ones were constructed in a tangented way like a figure eight. Square-plan tombs may also be found in any period, although the late stages had a special penchant for them, at which time they were fitted with a stone chamber on a level near the crest. In unusual cases three square mounds are lined up, the middle one larger than the other two. A square base may also act as a terrace and be the platform for a circular knoll.

The type most characteristic to Japan and through which the development of the entire period is traced is the circular mound with rectangular projection, referred to in Japanese as 'square front, round back' (*zempō-kōen*), resembling in shape a keyhole. To foil those who would trace the origins of this unique type to a little bump on the side of a tumulus that consistently enlarged in size, the beginnings are actually already quite pretentious, being a long, narrow, low mound. If this projection had increased in accordance with the extension of the chamber into the corridor type, the problem would hardly exist, but the corridor development belongs to the late stages of the Tomb period, and even so, the corridor is absorbed into either the knoll or the extension. One theory held by Suenaga and demon-strated in some cases, is that ends of hills were sliced off, or even cut into to isolate a mound, a point that is most reasonable simply because so many of the Early tombs are on hilltops and sides.[21] Another belief is that the projection is there to simulate an attached shrine, as in China, and, one might add, the psychology since Yayoi times had been to lengthen and widen, exactly what happens to this part of the tomb. Buhot, treating it more symbolically, believes it probably derived from the Chinese idea of the *hu*, in itself associated with the gourd.[22] While there must be some symbolism—or it must have de-veloped—the gourd-shaped tomb belongs to the last type only.

Plate 60

Chausuyama, Sakurai, Nara prefecture, is an excellent example of an Early tomb. The extension widens out only slightly, is considerably lower than the circular head. The moat has disappeared, but its outlines, made when earth was scooped out, are still visible. The excavation of the knoll revealed a pit-style stone chamber 21 feet long and about 5 feet high composed of numerous horizontally laid stones painted red, roofed by twelve long crossing slabs, also painted. The dead had been buried in a wooden coffin, around which the chamber was built. Chinese mirrors and a jade baton were among the objects retrieved.

Fig. 53a

By the fifth century the extension had almost reached the height of the round section, had widened to slightly greater than the diameter of the mound, and become defined in sharp angularity. In the vicinity, usually in four directions, were built small mounds, sometimes round, often square, or even keyhole-shaped. It used to be believed these were chiefly for immolations, or for members of the royal family or relatives, but Suenaga believes they were more intended for burial of relics.[23]

Plate 62

The grandest of these mausolea is the grave of Emperor

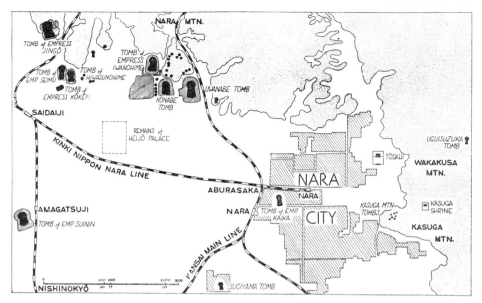

Map 6   Tombs in the vicinity of Nara city

Nintoku which lies on the Sakai Plain near Ōsaka amidst
a splendid array of thirteen smaller tombs. The group, including the tomb of Emperor Richū, numbers around twenty.
Nintoku's monument occupies eighty acres, having the total
length of 2,695 feet, from the outer edges of its three moats.
Little side blisters have appeared—too many and too regularly
placed in these tombs to be accidental—and may have supplanted the single shrine idea which had lost all meaning by
this time. Several years ago, a landslide that partially opened
this tomb yielded some of its treasures and exposed a magnificent
stone sarcophagus in the projecting section.

Obviously these tombs required a vast labour force working
for a considerable period to construct. The literature gives some
insights on the question. Nintoku, for instance, began his tomb
in his sixty-seventh year and lived twenty more years, clearly

151

sufficient time to complete even this huge undertaking. On the death of Emperor Chūai, it is said that since the country was at war with Silla the Emperor could not be buried, an unmasked reference to the great host of men required to build a tomb. Most emperors were interred a number of months after their death, probably to allow time for mourning, but also for tomb construction if necessary. A reference of double interest comes at the time Emperor Ingio died. When he heard it, the King of Silla sent eighty tribute ships loaded with mourners to the funeral, and nine months later the Emperor was buried near the Naniwa capital after all had assembled 'at the Shrine of temporary interment'.[24] Emperor Ankō was buried three years after his assassination.

Map 6

In some areas and at different times greater attention seems to have been shown in the orientation of the tombs. Outside Nara city, for instance, where the plateau rises, most of the large moat-surrounded tombs chiefly of the fourth century face south. Cut from the hills, quite a few actually follow the line of the ranges and thus a fixed direction is in part explained. Tombs attributed largely to fifth-century rulers, including the Ōjin

Map 7

colossus well out on the plain west of the Ishi River in the area of Furuichi city, Ōsaka prefecture, look quite helter-skelter, although a great many of the smaller moated mounds face south-west. A glance at one group, such as the thirty-three circular and keyhole tombs on Tamateyama, emphasizes the strangeness of this haphazard arrangement. Probably, however, variety now gave greater distinction, and more important than the orientation of the outward form was the direction of the chamber and body, often crossed through at a most unexpected angle, but generally in a southerly direction.

Towards the end of the Tomb period the projecting member of the keyhole tomb is approximately the height of the knoll and tends to be rounded at the end. Sizes have diminished, the moat frequently disappearing, and in fact hillside burials of the

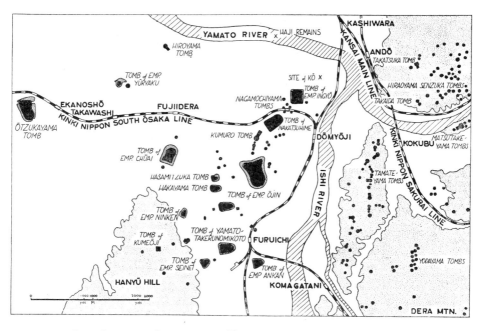

Map 7   Tombs in the vicinity of Furuichi city, Ōsaka prefecture

corridor type have eliminated the isolated barrow completely in many cases. Aerial views enhance the picturesqueness of these keyhole tombs whether in flooded rice paddy season or out. Radial lines within the old moat suit this shape, although its occupants would undoubtedly feel that much of its monumental splendour had been dissipated. The Nabeyama tomb contains a stone corridor entered through a hole in a house that lies transversally across the mound. Two housetype volcanic stone sarcophagi rest within the tomb, one in the chamber, the other in the passageway.

Plate 61

In the earliest tombs a hollowedout log using both halves served as a coffin. This was near the top of the mound where the earth was formed into a long rounded trench, banked on either side, surrounded by loose stones, or built up in a stone chamber

Plate 64

153

as support for the overhead soil. Sometimes two or more parallel trenches appear, and smaller trenches seem to have been for grave-goods. Coffins of thick wooden planks were also in vogue. This pit-style of burial was never fully discarded merely because it was the simplest and most economical of all the methods devised.

Coffins of more substantial materials are typical of the Middle period. Of the two main stone types, one resembles very closely the hollowed-out tree trunk, and may have rounded or vertically cut inner walls. The change is slight from log-shaped to boat-shaped sarcophagi, perhaps due to revised ideas concerning the transporting of the spirit of the dead. This kind is normally found in chambers of rather rough stones that are built only as tight-fitting envelopes to incorporate the sarcophagus, obviously finished after the housing of the coffin. The other is the house type, with some concurrence in use, but generally later in date and an accoutrement of fifth-century pit-type chambers and the succeeding corridor tombs where space may have permitted more than one to be placed. It is square in section, and its lid has the pitch of a house roof, sloping in four directions. There are many varieties, with rounded roof, flattened and so forth, but the basic form remains the same. Cases are known where the passage is too narrow for the sarcophagus to have been moved through, so it must have been deposited in the chamber before the completion of the corridor, or with the introduction of a second sarcophagus it was discovered that the constriction between hall and chamber was too small to permit passage of the sarcophagus, and without choice it was left in the corridor.

Much decoration is relatively rare on both stone types, but some carry simple moulding and strips like laths, and often resemble bamboo, and a few are represented by the well-known sarcophagus of Sekijinyama tomb in Fukuoka that is carved in complicated diagonal and circular patterns. Several are

Plates 65, 66

Plate 72

painted red. The house type may be chiselled out of one block as its predecessor had been, but is more often composed of six separate slabs, five neatly jointed, and in rare cases even more. There are lugs on the sides and ends, round in most earlier examples, often square in later ones, and the very latest stone sarcophagi may have none. Quite a number of the house-shaped ones from many sections of Japan have regular holes cut through the sides or ends through which the corpse or a later addition to the grave must have been slid—particularly if the chamber was too cramped for removal of the lid. Also, when there was direct sarcophagus burial in a mound without benefit of a chamber, this was frequently the case; the huge stone sarcophagus could be put in place, then a wooden coffin pushed into it through the hole. Direct sarcophagi burials almost all date to late years in the Tomb period.

There is another variety that is often more a part of the actual chamber construction: long slabs arranged as cist-like boxes. It is perhaps more common in South Japan. The Marukumayama tomb with its Siamese-twin cists of one common slab has space for two; and Ōtsuka tomb of Okayama has cists like enclosure screens both at the end and the side.

Plate 69

Fig. 35a

In early centuries of cremation the removal of stone sarcophagi must have been quite a pastime, as their presence today in so many unexpected places illustrates. They may be seen in temple grounds, in gardens as basins, cut and used like conduits, or serving as troughs; the lids may be standing as grave markers in cemeteries, be acting as bridges between rice paddies, and elsewhere. One famous sarcophagus in Futai temple, Nara city, has numerous depressions along its rim where generations of farmers apparently sharpened their sickles. Many of these in the Kansai are of tufa from Mount Futagami on the border between Ōsaka and Nara and in all likelihood are the work of a small number of workshops specializing in the art.

Clay coffins achieved their greatest popularity in the Oka-yama and Hyōgo region (Inland Sea), but a few have been found in the Kansai, Kantō, and as far north as Fukushima prefecture. Strangely enough, in Kyūshū, where one would have expected the potters to have trained themselves while making Yayoi funeral jars, this idea never took hold. On the whole the clay ones follow their stone cousins fairly closely; the house type of curved or pitched roof with panelled wall effects is the most common. In the same red clay as the *haniwa*, these are made in four sections, have the usual lid lugs, and look quite centipedal with as many as thirty short tubular legs in three rows. Low sculptured relief designs may be seen on the end of one from Okayama. Generally speaking, these are rather late coffins, since many come from hillside stone chambers or rock-cut caves or were direct burials. For some of the very last tombs that actually correspond to the Hakuhō era (A.D. 673–86) dry lacquer coffins were provided, an expensive luxury that must have been deplored by the Buddhist segment of society adjusting itself to cremation.

Plate 63

Adults could also be interred in a cylinder of clay, capped at both ends, slightly reminiscent of the old Yayoi jar burials. In cases where two cylindrical *haniwa* were used, the usual circular holes may be seen. The capped ones are normally closely ribbed. A child might get special treatment and be entombed in a moccasin-shaped coffin, although this was a rare child indeed.

Many stone sarcophagi have had a head-rest carved into them, often two for head-to-foot occupancy, or side by side in the cist-type settings. There are frequent references in the literature to joint burial, particularly of husband and wife, often described as done for economy's sake, and undoubtedly the corridor tombs were designed with multiple burials in view. Separate stone pillows are usually later than built-in ones, and were preferred in the Tōkai and Kantō, whereas the

Plate 66

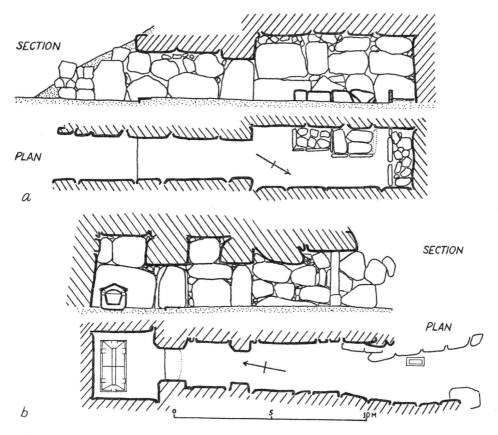

Fig. 35 Diagrams of corridor tombs: (a) Ōtsuka tomb, Yata, Okayama, (b) Ayatsuka tomb, Miyako county, Fukuoka

latter took precedence in the more southerly areas. Loose and fixed head-rests appear together in the same tomb, however, as in the painted Ōtsuka tomb, Fukuoka, and in such circumstances may be taken as a way of recognizing the different social status of those buried therein. Loose pillows take a variety of forms, from a simple depression in a cylindrical stone to an elaborately hollowed-out and decorated ornamental piece.

Stone chambers were built in either the knoll of the tomb or the rectangular extension, and there are cases where both have chambers, or two are located in one end. A war-time discovery in the Kurohimeyama tomb, Kawachi Plain, Ōsaka prefecture, showed that the front and back rooms had no connecting corridor: one was for burial of the dead exclusively, the other for arms, armour and miscellaneous paraphernalia.

Fig. 35b

The typical stone passage-way of Late tombs widens into a chamber, or may even consist of a sequence of three rooms, though more common is a sort of ante-chamber. Rooms are rarely alike in height and floor measurement. In a simple corbelled vault the upper part of the walls is inclined inwards in order to shorten the distance to be spanned by the lintels. Many types of construction were used, the narrow horizontal courses being a carry-over from the earlier chamber that was nothing more than a sarcophagus case. The kind one sees most is a construction in large roughly hewn stones of impressive scale, the interstices filled with smaller stones. Variations naturally depend on regions and availability of materials, and skills improved less rapidly in provincial areas.

Plate 67, 68

It is generally believed that the corridor tomb is also a reflection of continental practices and had its beginnings in Kyūshū. Most of these are designed to open towards the south, and there is a preference for the head to be placed in the same direction within the burial chamber. By the end of the period some superb results were being achieved in stone cutting and fitting, the most justly well known being the West tomb of Monjuin, Nara prefecture, where granite blocks of many sizes sloping towards the ceiling are cut with surface grooves to make it appear as though the blocks overlap on alternate courses. The corridor has near its entrance a furrow in an overhead stone, a sign of some sort of door originally, and the chamber is covered with one huge slab, slightly arched internally in order to carry leaking water to and down the four corners rather than permitting it to streak the walls. A standing Buddhist Fudō image is apparently centuries old.

The mightiest of all, now exposed, traditionally known as Ishibutai ('Stone stage'), stands below an incline not far from some of the old Asuka temples near Shimanoshō, Nara prefecture. Its stripping and looting probably took place a thousand years ago, but its excavation was conducted in 1935. A moat banked with stones surrounded the entire square-shaped tomb, the corridor and chamber more or less in the middle. To give some idea of size, the former is 38 feet long and its stones average 6 feet in height; the chamber is 25 feet long, 11 wide and $15\frac{1}{2}$ at its highest point. Although intended by design, it surprises the modern visitor as much as it must have pleased the ancient builders to see the unusual degree of juxtaposition on the inner surfaces of the great boulders. The floor slopes slightly and has been given side gutters so that water runs to the back, and then out by a centre ditch which is underground in the chamber, but exposed in the corridor. The two gigantic stones that make up the roof have been estimated to be 100 tons each, and all the materials were brought down from a mountain quarry about two miles away. One tradition claims this to be the tomb of a Minister of Shima, Soga-no-Umako by name, who died in A.D. 626, and undoubtedly in a technical sense the Ishibutai is extremely late in the development and could well be of the seventh century.

Plates 70, 71

There are places in Japan noted for their hillside rock-cut caves. The majority have an entrance-way that could be closed by a door, and a short corridor that narrows to an opening into a roughly rectangular chamber. The Yoshimi group, Saitama, consists of more than two hundred, dotting the sloping cliff as close as excavation would permit. Inside most are two or three low platforms with head-rests on which the bodies must have been placed, and investigations in the nineteenth century revealed all sorts of beads, iron swords, knives and arrowheads, gold rings and Tomb period Sue-style pottery. Pottery coffins are sometimes found in these, and the Takaida cave of Nakakawachi county, Ōsaka, has wall scratchings of tunic and trousered figures dressed in a familiar *haniwa* style.

New requirements of economy and an eventual turning to the Buddhist practice of cremation brought the final demise of the tumulus burial for all but the immediate imperial family. The decrees of Emperor Kōtoku of A.D. 646 are prefaced by the remark, 'Of late, the poverty of our people is absolutely owing to the construction of tombs'.[25] Except for imperial tombs, the size was regulated by decree: for princes and upwards '. . . the work shall be completed by 1,000 labourers in seven days', and four other categories of ranks were graded accordingly. 'The construction of places of temporary inter ment is not allowed in any case, from Princes down to common people.' No valuables were to be buried with the dead and burials were to be in cemeteries set apart for the purpose. It would appear that not all tumulus building ceased immedi ately, even though the decree went out to every province; most effective in bringing its end was the full-scale adoption of cremation.

THE CONTENTS OF TOMBS

Fig. 36a

The preferred arrangement of funerary objects was near the body, weapons to either side, armour towards the head or, in a case like the Sando tomb, Kyōto prefecture, the helmet, armour and arrowheads were outside the sarcophagus for lack of space within. The flooring of this sarcophagus was a $3\frac{1}{2}$-inch bed of small stones. The famous Choshi-zuka of Ikisan, Fukuoka, built in the latter half of the fourth century and containing a wooden coffin within a stone chamber, illustrated

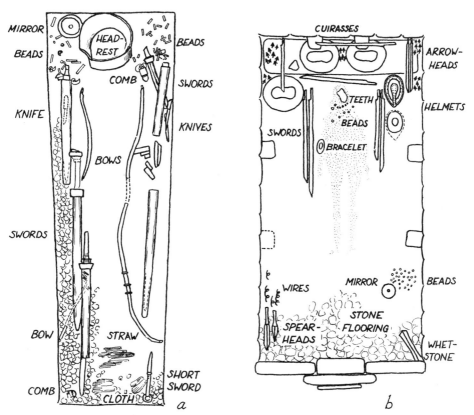

Fig. 36 Arrangement of grave-goods in tombs: (a) Sando tomb, Takeno, Kyōto, (b) Tokumaru tomb, Chitose, Fukuoka

in a most graphic way the magical use of the mirror: ten mirrors were regularly arranged, four to a side, two at the head, surrounding the upper part of the corpse in a closely protecting position. A number of swords, knives and beads were also discovered. In many tombs great quantities of pottery were often placed at the foot, sometimes on wooden shelves that eventually collapsed, scattering the pieces in a jumble.

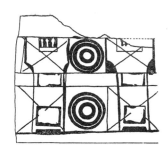

Fig. 37   Wall and stone screen designs in tombs: (a) Idera tomb, Rokka, Kumamoto, (b) Segonkō I tomb, Oshima, Kumamoto. Height of design about 18"

Ante-rooms are used for pottery as well, although a completely separate room may be specially designed to house grave-goods.

North Kyūshū has between forty and fifty decorated tombs, mostly of the Late corridor type, that are either carved or painted or occasionally both, dating to between A.D. 500 and 700. These are heavily allocated to the sixth century. The proximity to Korea is indication of the source of the practice, but connections with the Korean painted tombs in subject-matter are unexpectedly slight. In certain cases the sarcophagi, cist screens, and side walls share designs in common, the most popular being red concentric circles that represent either mirrors or suns, or both. Other abstract motifs include intersecting diagonal and curved lines (*chokkomon*), a complicated design that permeates all the arts after spreading from the Kansai—mirrors, bracelets, *haniwa*, sword guards and others—whose meaning must be magical but is still a mystery; triangles, and a very limited repertoire of geometric shapes. More recognizable are the horses, quivers, swords, knives, and a frequently recurring motif that resembles a starfish with tails. Due to the emphasis placed on isolated designs and the value ascribed to repetition, there can be little question that these have magical powers, and should provide an atmosphere conducive to

Fig. 37

protection by benign spirits. The concentric circles are less precisely used than in Korean tombs, partly because construction of the chamber had not yet reached a stage that provided the artist with flat unbroken surfaces, but more because the idea of design in art was still on a purely primitive level. These starfish tails, mentioned above, often appear quite separately, but the motif, even though oriented in various directions, may very well be a ceremonial fan representing status, and borrowed indirectly from China.

The Ōtsuka tomb in Fukuoka is the most elaborately painted example, singularly displaying decoration in both forechamber and main chamber. Two miniature figures on black horses flank the entrance to the main room; the same wall on the main chamber side has fourteen large quivers; its other walls carry ten on one side and eleven visible shields on the other, and triangles filling the spaces. An alcove designed for two bodies was covered by an overhead shelf; two stones were placed in front on which lamps were burned for the interment ceremonies. These stones bear fan patterns, and most of the

Plate 73

BLUE   RED   WHITE

Fig. 38   Painted ceremonial fan on walls of Kamao tomb Nishisato, Kumamoto

Plates 74, 75

Fig. 39   Painting on wall of Mezurashi tomb, Fukutomi, Fukuoka

Fig. 40 Design of boat on wall of Onizuka tomb, Imi, Ōita

Fig. 39

wall surfaces in immediate proximity to the corpse receptacle are covered with small triangles in yellow, black, red and green colours.

In only a few instances is there an attempt to describe an activity or event in the wall paintings. The Gōroyama tomb, Fukuoka, along with bows, quivers and circles, has a number of crudely painted hunters with drawn bows, and four-legged animals as targets. The state of preservation is not good, but it is clear that one hunter and perhaps two are on horseback; nevertheless, the composition and proportion of the figures have made no noticeable progress since Yayoi bell-relief designs and pottery incising. The most advanced in design is a painting in the Takehara tomb which appears to show a man being attacked by two animals; large fans stand on either side. More involved, but not in narrative treatment, is the Mezurashi tomb painting, also in Fukuoka, where an ensemble of suns, quivers and spirals is combined with other signs. A boat appears to be under sail; the crow on its bow is two-legged as against the Korean three-legged crow which is a sun symbol, and a frog at the other end may be a moon symbol.

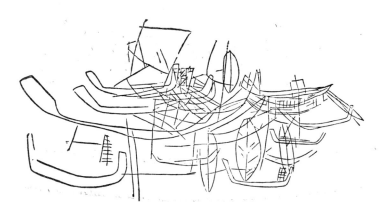

Fig. 41   Incised boats on wall of rock-cut tomb at Midorikawa, Kumamoto

Fig. 42   Detail of incised men and boats on wall of rock-cut tomb at Takaida, Kashiwara, Ōsaka

Interestingly enough, boats play a rather prominent role in subject-matter in several tombs, and more than likely are associated with the transporting of the soul of the deceased to another land. Onizuka in Ōita has a boat that would seem to be using sails, and scratched on the west wall of the Midori-kawa tomb, Kumamoto, a sailing-boat is clearly enough de-picted, but the antiquity of the work has been questioned. On the opposite wall, like the last of hard andesite, an entire fleet of ten or more craft are rendered in an almost futuristic fashion. One or two may have unfurled sails, but the leaf-shaped objects are most likely oars, if one can judge by illu-strations elsewhere. The *haniwa* boat from Miyazaki eliminates the guess-work in many respects. All the boats are of the usual gondola type, but seamen are conspicuously absent. Just the opposite is the case in a wall incising in the passageway of a rock-cut tomb at Takaida, Kashiwara, Ōsaka prefecture, a detail of which is shown. Six men frontally disposed wear similar costumes and tall hats; of these, three brandish spears. At least one is on a boat, and perhaps another, but the picture

Fig. 40

Fig. 41

Plate 102

Fig. 42

165

fades out. It comes as a reminder of a task force with an amphibious unit. The detail indicates the boat can be propelled by one oar, and one heavy stone is used for an anchor.

Kumamoto prefecture has a number of rockcut vaults of probably sixth century date in which cliffsides by the entranceways are carved in coarse, low, flattened relief sculptures. Two men appear at the Nabeta village tomb; one is shown frontally, holding his bow pointed towards himself, while the other is seen from the back in a crossshaped pattern. Independent sculptures prove that this is the customary manner of representing the back of a figure with quiver attached. This man probably actually operates the bow with drawn arrow on the left. Below is another type of quiver, and the circle between the two men is a *tomo*, the archer's aid, and possibly the unfinished looking object underneath is a fourlegged beast, the quarry. Vault 7 at Ōmura, believed to be one of the earliest of these, seems to be an attempt at depicting horses on two registers; an upper one at least is saddled. A longeared creature below looks more like an ass, and to the left the suspended objects are probably one small and two very much enlarged horse bells.

Body armour is very well known as a result of striking finds from many tombs and the additional light that *haniwa* models throw on the subject. The most common iron type was a cuirass or corselet of horizontal, overlapping bands riveted together and reinforced with vertical strips along the sides. The *haniwa* suggest that somewhat similar ones in leather could be tied in the front, and shoulder protectors were fairly customary. More elaborate was the complete covering, manifested by a magnificent example from Nagamochiyama, Ōsaka prefecture. Small plates of iron were held in place by leather thongs. Not shown in the illustration are the arm and leg guards, as well as the cheekpieces and neck protector of the helmet.

Plate 76

Plate 77

Fig. 43c

Fig. 43b

Plate 78

Two helmet types were made in iron; one frequently seen with the cuirass is the kind just mentioned: oval in the back and sharp-edged at the front. The other is round, and is often supplied with ornamented visor and a cup-shaped plume holder on the top. Both types probably were normally equipped with neck protectors, and may have had attached cheek-pieces.

Plate 79

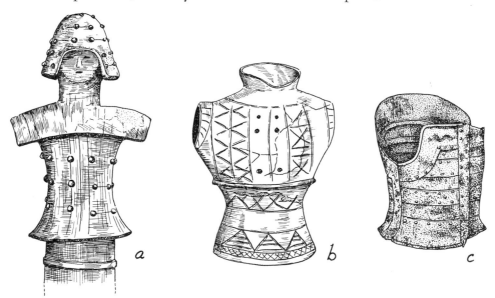

Fig. 43 Iron cuirass and haniwa *armour: (a) Tatsukawa, Gumma, (b) Shimomasuda, Miyagi, about 16″, (c) Kisa, Hiroshima*

The great attention usually devoted to the gilding and decorating of this type in patterns of fish, birds and animals must mean it had a special rank significance. There is unquestionably much continental influence in the arms and armour of the period, but the bizarre and fantastic character of the creatures engraved on the bands seems to be entirely of Japanese artistry.

The helmeted *haniwa* figures are far more varied than the two iron types, and must tell the story not only of the metal

Fig. 44

but also of the leather head-pieces. The latter, of course, are strongly under the influence of the metal models, but it seems doubtful to me that any of those illustrated—and a cross-section is—could actually be mythical. Some would appear to be more practical than others, and it may be reasonable to look on certain ones as being largely of a ceremonial nature. Most of this armour is production of the Middle Tomb period, and the

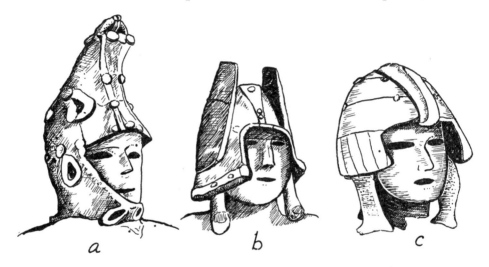

Fig. 44 Helmets illustrated by the haniwa: (*a*) *Sawa county, Gumma,* (*b*) *Minowa, Gumma,*

method of linking together small rectangles of iron did not make its appearance until the latter half of the fifth century.

The long single-edged sword originally of Han Dynasty China was much preferred over the short sword by the Yamato people, partly because of its greater psychological value. As many as fourteen long ones have been found in a tomb, and ten or so is not at all uncommon. Some are handsomely

Fig. 46

sheathed in gold-covered and -embossed cases, their handles bound with gold wire. The ring-handled variety was intro- duced from Korea, and true to form, goes on to new heights.

The Korean trefoil pattern and three-arc handles are exceedingly rare discoveries in Japan, but the dragon heads and bird
heads, either singly, *tête-à-tête* or back to back, known in
Korea, are relatively plentiful in Japan. One that is extremely
Chinese in appearance is an animal face in front view, seen in
several examples. The confronted heads holding a ball is the
most elaborate type, and is frequently gilt. There is no reason

Plate 81

Fig. 45

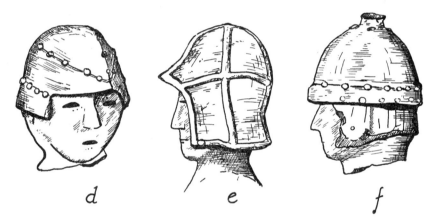

(*c, d*) *uncertain*, (*e*) *Chibata, Shizuoka*, (*f*) *Chūjō, Saitama*

for thinking it is not a misunderstood Buddhist motif that
enters the country in a well-intentioned and rather realistic
way, but proceeds to exhibit perfectly the Japanese talent for
abstracting a basic design. As time progresses, and in this case
in the regions of Okayama, Mie and Chiba, the profile heads
are flattened out and become increasingly stylized and decorative. The book of *Six Codes* of T'ang Dynasty China refers to
ornamental handles for ceremonial swords, and these in Japan
may be a reflection of this, although Chinese originals fitting
the description have not yet been noted. The Korean examples

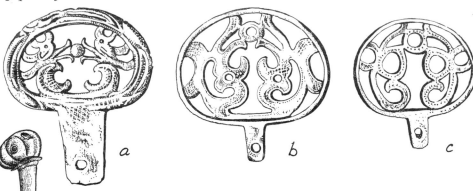

*Fig. 45 Dragon-headed sword pommels: (a) Kuse, Okayama, length 3½",
(b) Yokkaichi, Mie, length 3 7/16", (c) Iino, Chiba, length 2 7/8"*

are from Silla. The second half of the seventh century in Japan
sees the use of the round-pommelled sword, also exotically gilt
in most instances.

Plate 80

The three main stemmed arrowhead types in bronze are
particularly prevalent in the Early Tomb period and may be
found together. Less frequent is the paper-thin type with central
perforation, triangularly indented base and short stem that
projects only as far as the lower points; and a stemless variety
whose striking end has convex outlines, the body concave
sides and a thin membrane across a U-shaped depression.

Shields are such familiar designs in tombs that the standard

Fig. 47b

shape of arched top and slightly curved sides is well known. A
mirror with a lot of little men illustrates shields as being large

Fig. 47c

and in the form of an arc, but many things about the mirror are
thoroughly beserk. Rectangular iron shields of metal strips
riveted together are found amongst grave-goods, but had little
practical use, since they stood around four feet in height and
were awkward in weight. These must have been the kind
which are referred to as awards made by imperial authority.

*Fig. 46 Iron sword
with gold fittings from
Niihari, Ibaragi.
Length about 44"*

Fig. 47 Shields and shield ornaments: (a) reconstructed shield from Sakurazuka tomb, Toyonaka city, Ōsaka, (b) wall painting in Ōtsuka tomb, Fukuoka, (c) from mirror with hunting figures from Gumma, (d, e) ornaments from Kinrei tomb, Kisarazu city, Chiba, (f, g) uncertain

More useful would be those in wood and leather, the leather ones perhaps lacquered or brocaded, as attested by the coloured remains of one from Sakurazuka tomb, Toyonaka city, Ōsaka. Circular, floral and whirl ornaments of bronze now seem to have been fixtures for the shields, serving a partially ornamental purpose.

Fig. 47a

Fig. 47d–g

The portable quiver was in most cases strapped to the back, a manner borne out by the *haniwa* and stone sculptures, and is the kind normally pictured in tomb paintings, but several *haniwa* also represent colossal arrow holders, all too similar to be mythical, which equal the height of a man, and were in all probability of wood. One can only conjecture that they would have been hauled out by two or more labourers, not only for the approved diversion of target practice, but also may have been carried in processions and done their duty in archery contests and associated ceremonies as well. Interestingly enough, they, like many others, show that the arrows were stacked with points up.

Fig. 48a

Fig. 48c

Stone copies of knives, daggers, arrowheads and assorted other arms and armour from tombs are in some instances part

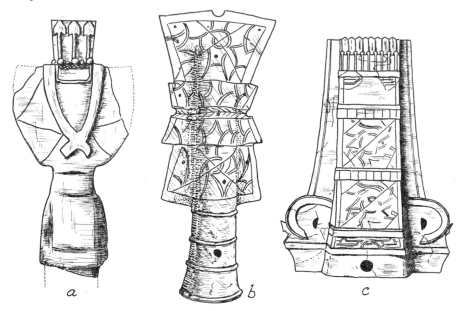

Fig. 48 Haniwa *quivers: (a) Gōdo, Gumma, about 26″, (b) Miyake, Nara, about 46½″, (c) Okubo, Kyōto, about 42″*

Fig. 49f–h

of the psychology that believes the power of the magical spell is proportional to the number of charms—a psychology to which the *magatama* collectors are the most conspicuous subscribers. In the Katonboyama tomb, Sakai city, literally scores of miniature sheathed knives about an inch and a half in length came to light, comparable to those illustrated. The little curved knives here and hanging at the waists of *haniwa* men are in their leather cases so the exact shape is left to the imagination, but this kind undoubtedly had a wide, single-edged cleaver-like blade. There is as yet no satisfactory explanation why the blades were virtually always hidden.

The rapidly rising popularity of the horse in the second half of the fifth century forced the emphasis on the foot soldier's personal armour to give way to the need for horse trappings, and related paraphernalia of the mounted warrior. Body armour did not immediately disappear, but it was hardly compatible with the actual and psychological requirements of the horse-riding gentry of the earlier half of the Late Tomb period. The sixth century, to which the *haniwa* horses and tomb represen-tations belong, was a noteworthy phase of florescence in the arts. The country was on the threshold of transformation to Buddhism, and as the guilds were accumulating traditions and increasing skills to meet the demands made on them by the wealthy class to provide objects of artistic value for the tombs, they were also unwittingly preparing themselves for a repertoire that eventually was needed to produce the furni-ture for Buddhist temples. Thus, although in the late sixth and early seventh centuries Korean workmen had to be brought in —as had been done frequently before—this time to act as tutors for the completely foreign icons and other equipment of

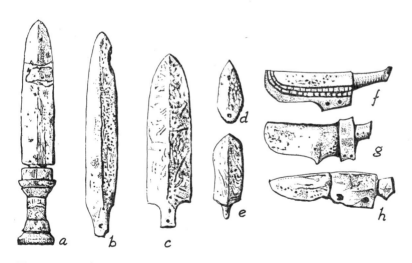

Fig. 49   Stone daggers, arrowheads and knives from tombs: (a) Miromi, Gifu, (b, f) Kawai, Nara, (c) Gumma, (d) Yokokawa, Tochigi, (e) Umami, Nara, (g) Minami-tachibana, Gumma, (h) Iwahana, Gumma

Buddhist worship places, the change-over in many respects was not a difficult one. For example, it was a simple matter for the grey pottery makers to switch from ceremonial ware for tombs to tiles for temples.

Upheavals on the continent at the time furnish the background details for the native sixth-century renaissance. It would seem that a people of strong Turkish strain, probably not too distantly removed from the earlier Wei of China, had come through Korea and now composed the dominant group of the upper class. They were closely akin to the Silla aristocracy through frequent intermarriage, and had reproduced much of the atmosphere of the mother country in the new land. Egami sees certain fundamental traits in the protohistoric period as having an Inner Asian origin, and has suggested that the changes were directly caused by pastoral warriors arriving in Kyūshū and imposing themselves as rulers on an agricultural society.[26] The plausibility of this thesis is greater if one can accept a series of migrations of horse riders from the steppes (a very likely thing), the bulk not arriving until towards the sixth century when the predominant horse-riding character took over; otherwise the scattered and successive appearance of the Inner Asian features in the Tomb culture are not satisfactorily explained.

Fig. 50   Horse in silver inlay on iron sword from Funayama tomb, Kikusui, Kumamoto

Plate 101

The ring-handled sword is a constant companion to these horse trappings, although its early history in Japan antedates the mass of the horse equipment by fifty or more years, and both later disappear around the middle of the seventh century. It is interesting to recognize familiar details in relief sculptures from the China mainland that illustrate baggy trousered males, cousins to the *haniwa*, who are armed with comparable swords.

The *haniwa* once again are useful in ascertaining the manner of harnessing the horse and the arrangement of ornamental accoutrements. Artistically the *haniwa* horses represent the creatures as amiable, silent guardians, transfixed and immobile, but suggestive of controlled or latent power that could well spring to life at any moment. On the other hand, a running horse in silver inlay on the handle of a sword from Kumamoto is shown in a rare burst of movement. The technique in this case is little more than mediocre, but its crudities endow the steed with a primitive energy quite unseen in other representa-tions. The spiral patterns on the flanks may owe their existence to indirect Scythian connections.

Fig. 50

Bridle-bits range from the extremely simple and unorna-mented to gold-plated S-shaped cheek-pieces that also imply distant Scythian influence. Similarly, the realism so prominent in the floral patterns of the latter half of the Late Tomb period draws heavily from Sui and early T'ang China, although those of greater stylization are more characteristically Japanese. *Haniwa* and several actual discoveries represent the typical stirrup as round or oval in shape, occasionally flattened under the foot. The *haniwa* horse without stirrups is unusual, and one creature even has a damaged and shapeless object that seems to be an attempt to represent the gilt bronze pocket stirrup of late date. Examples rather similar to the one from Fukuoka are today the property of the Shōsōin and Hōryūji.

Frontispiece

Fig. 51 Gilt bronze stirrup from Miyajigoku Shrine grounds, Fukuoka

What remains of the saddles in the tombs are frequently ornamented arcs of metal that made up front and rear pieces. The shape of the *haniwa* saddle has little in common with the long Wei saddle, but does show some connection with the more neighbouring Silla type.

The rich variety of pendants are also excellently portrayed in the *haniwa*. Frequently gilt and cast in intricate open-work, they simulate miniature saddles of more or less square shape, repro-duce the continental heart or floral patterns, or are variations of circles, ovals, lozenges, or combinations of the circular and pentagonal forms. Little spherical bronze or gold bells were attached to the straps of the head, neck and flanks of the horse, and large bells dangled at the breast. Bells indentical to those

Fig. 52

Plate 82

Plate 84

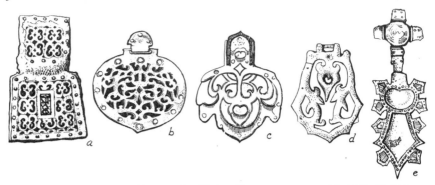

Fig. 52   Horse ornaments: (a) Furuichi, Ōsaka, (b) Tsuma, Miyagi, (c) Meiji, Tochigi, (d) Saitama, Saitama, (e) Ōtsuka tomb, Fukuoka

Plate 83

Fig. 53b–d

illustrated were discovered in the Mendori tomb of a village by the same name in Ehime prefecture, Shikoku. Used in another way at either the cheek or breech, the spherical bells were affixed to the outer edges of a circular ring or disc or to a plate covered with minute bosses, such as the example from Shin-taku, Saitama. The result bears much resemblance to those bronze mirrors which carry little bells.

Among the deposits in the Early tombs is an unusual assort-ment of carved and perfectly finished stone objects whose exact significance remains a troublesome question. At once they resemble stylized figurines, sword handles, parasitical *magatama* on a truncated sword, feebly disguised phallic symbols, and a host of other articles—imaginary or real. It should be pointed out that almost all have two legs, sometimes diminished to just a fish-tail heel (Fig. 53c is atypical), and certain other features in common. Whether coincidentally or not, the preponderance of these in Early tombs in the Kansai region shares the same distribution as the 'hoe-shaped' bracelets.

Morimoto feels that these stones are all derived from one source that is quite Japanese, but not entirely free from con-tinental influence. Basing his theory on the fact that a carved

176

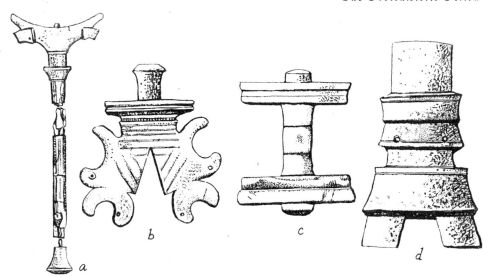

Fig. 53 Stone objects from tombs: (a) Chausuyama tomb, Nara, 19½", (b, c) Maruyama tomb, Tomio, Nara, (d) Ishigami, Nara (b) 2⅜", (c) and (d) to same scale

plectrum-shaped implement of antler was found in a corridor tomb, he suggests they are therefore highly stylized versions of the separate bridges placed under each string of the *koto*, a musical instrument mentioned in the early literature and played by *haniwa* figures.[27] The plectrum, incidentally, for plucking the *samisen*, a guitar-like instrument, appears as a *haniwa* in itself. The stone object from the Early Chausuyama tomb has been identified as a symbol of authority. It is sword-shaped, knobbed at one end, and provided with a useless grip or handle at the other, reinforced throughout by an iron rod.

Fig. 53a

Replicas of shell and metal bracelets in stone must have had much value in quantitative terms: a tomb in Akasaka, Gifu, yielded fifty-four circular bracelets and one hoe-shaped example; a Tsuzuki county tomb, Kyōto prefecture, contained a total of eleven in four different types. Stone bracelets may come in sets of graded sizes, and are often painted red. The annular ones

Fig. 54

Fig. 54a

are the most profuse and widespread. The type that resembles a sword-guard takes a number of variations, but most interesting is the so-called hoe-shaped bracelet. Strange legends associate it with the fox, the rice god, Inari, but this appears to have to do originally with one having been dug up by a fox, and is obviously a most superficial relationship. It is quite likely an

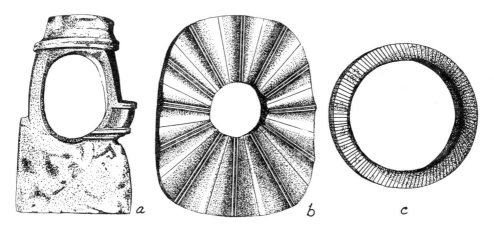

Fig. 54 *Stone bracelets from tombs: (a) Maruyama tomb, Tomio, Nara, (b) uncertain, (c) Yawata-machi tomb, Kyōto, diam. 3″*

enlarged and deformed piece of archery equipment that has now lost all features by which one can identify its origins and derivation with certainty.

Korean immigrants brought with them ornamental head-gear and may have been responsible for developing an aware-ness among the native people of its attractions—attractions that are testified to by the *haniwa* and tomb remains. The small gilt

Plate 85

headpiece from the Funayama tomb of Kumamoto, wrought in intricate animal patterns of open-work and with a kind of crest holder attached, is without doubt Korean made. This kind is believed to have been used in conjunction with a crown, as was the case in the southern area of the peninsula. Tall vertical

crowns are found in Gumma, Fukui, Chiba, Shiga, Ehime
and elsewhere, and one fine example is composed of three,
armed tree-like formations, and all may bear small dangling
magatama or discs suspended by gold wires, quite comparable
to those of Mimana and Silla and implying that the connection
these have with Korea is very direct. The *haniwa*, too, illustrate

Fig. 64

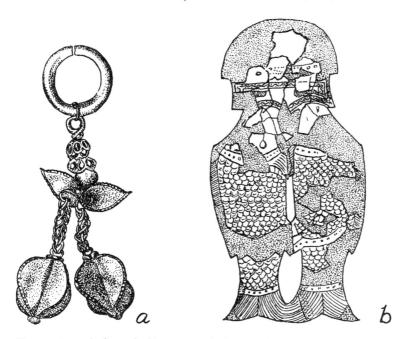

Fig. 55 One each of pair of gold ear-rings and gilt bronze fish pendants: (a) Kamoinari-
yama tomb, Mizuo, Shiga, 2⅜", (b) Kiyokawa, Kisarazu city, Chiba, 8 1/16"

a magnificent assortment of head-dresses, some of which are
crowns.

Gilt bronze shoes also have their Korean counterparts, and
lead one to believe that their owners had quite lately arrived, for
not a few instances of members of a Korean royal house residing in
Japan are mentioned in the texts. Most of the hanging ornaments

Plate 86

are now missing from these shoes, but they even included miniature fish dangling from the soles. No *haniwa* illustrate footgear of this nature, so their ceremonial value must have been primarily sepulchral, but they were a luxury out of reach of all but the titled, and too foreign for the majority of the élite.

Fig. 55

Ear-rings and waist ornaments belong to the volume of personal adornments entombed with the dead in the sixth century. The close identity that these also have with Korean examples shows that nothing new has changed the thinking

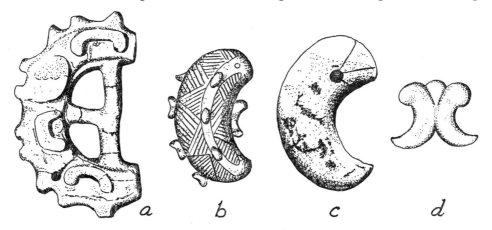

Fig. 56   Stone magatama *from tombs:* (a) *Kanegasaki tomb, Matsue city, Shimane,* (b) *Uchiura, Shizuoka,* $3\frac{1}{4}''$, (c) *near Emperor Nintoku's tomb, Sakai, Ōsaka,* $2\frac{3}{8}''$, (d) *Kagamizuka tomb, Isohama, Ibaragi*

since Hamada and Umehara considered them along with the bronze shoes to be either Korean in origin or made in Japan by migrant Korean craftsmen.[28] Ostentatious display of ear pendants was barbarous to the Chinese, but Silla people had such a passion for hanging ornaments, displaying them as pendants, jingling beads, hearts, discs and other items sus-pended from an assortment of objects including grey tomb pottery, that one might facetiously characterize them as fab-ricators of a 'dangling culture'. The technical treatment of these ear-rings is of the highest quality, and the filigree work on some must surely indicate Korean manufacture. The gilt fish were waist pendants that the Chinese of T'ang times are known to have appreciated, and a belief in their nature as talismans was probably already an old tradition in the countries of the Far East. With regard to these fish, the tomb replicas of Korea and Japan may reach the remarkable length of eight inches.

Ancient symbols cannot be discussed without making mention of the *magatama*, the curved bead that played such an important role in the protection of the descendants of the Sun Goddess. It had already developed some value as a charm in the Jōmon period, and though not too prevalent in Yayoi times and almost completely unknown in the great Yayoi sites, it blossoms out in a vast and fascinating array of forms and materials in the Tomb period, perhaps under renewed Korean inspiration. Instances occur of collections of hundreds in one tomb. In almost any available stone as well as in glass, a *magatama* sometimes assumes surprising proportions of several inches in length. In their variety, they are composite, back-to-back, piggy-back (or 'mother and child' by Japanese termino-logy), and subsidiary to a number of other objects.

Amongst the pottery debris in the Kinrei tomb of Kisarazu, Chiba, and behind the sarcophagus were two flat, gilt bronze perforated plates. Their position in the chamber suggested that they had been on a wooden shelf along with pottery. One of these was badly smashed, but the other is intact except for broken edges and missing pendants. They have been recog-nized as ceremonial fans to which something like feathers and a long handle were attached, and whose slow movement would have resulted in a pleasant tinkling sound that was designed to ward off evil spirits lurking in the vicinity. The trumpet-shaped patterns in the open-work and evidence gathered else-where in the tomb make a seventh-century date for the assem-bled objects a strong probability. In passing it might be noted

Fig. 56

Fig. 57 Gilt bronze fan from Kinrei tomb, Kisarazu city, Chiba. Length 12¼"

181

that this exceedingly rich tomb had already yielded gilt bronze shoes in 1932, and the 1950 excavations brought out from the sarcophagus and chamber horse furniture in the form of three incomplete saddles and assorted metal fittings, as well as body armour and a helmet, ring-handled iron swords, numerous bronze bells and small gold bells, silver bow tips, gold laces, two bronze vessels, one mirror originally on the chest of the deceased, hundreds of beads, and about 210 pieces of pottery.

Fig. 38
Fig. 58a

To return to the fan: the ceremonial fan is identified in tomb paintings and in the *haniwa*, where it may have a circular or serrated edge, the latter rarely well preserved. Ceremonial fans lend dignity to aristocratic figures in Wei Buddhist relief sculptures in China, and were introduced to Japan in two forms, although in the process neither seems to have been very strikingly coloured by local imagination. The *haniwa* ones, however, are at least a century earlier than these bronze examples, and must be a variation of an oblong-shaped type of fifth-century China, whereas the Kinrei tomb fans follow another of the same century that may be seen in carvings in the Buddhist caves of Lung Men.

Fig. 58b

In the same vein is the *haniwa* sunshade, this time assuming a much more picturesque and at the same time unlikely look, but probably representing a rather large though still portable parasol not too different from that pointed out on the mirror with four buildings. Scroll paintings of the procession for the transfer ceremony at Ise Shrine show marchers carrying shades with turned up frills around the edge and decorative patterns. The exuberant flourishes are not entirely fantastic, but are still exaggerated if one judges by the illustrations. The omnipresent *chokkomon* ornaments a number. The archer's *tomo*, the hollow bulb that aids him in the discharge of his arrow and magnifies its humming sound, is often seen hanging at the waist of the sculptured warriors. Enlarged many times its normal size, it also became a respectable *haniwa* subject.

Fig. 58c

The *haniwa* swords put new light on problems that have to do with objects not actually deposited in tombs. They resemble a small hand-operated fire extinguisher, have a guard that pro-tects the back of the hand, and are invariably shown encased in long tubular sheaths. Nothing of this nature has been found in bronze or iron in the tombs, so they could not have been the type for normal use, as Gotō points out.[29] He recognizes the relationship between these and the Sengūshiki ceremony at

Fig. 58d

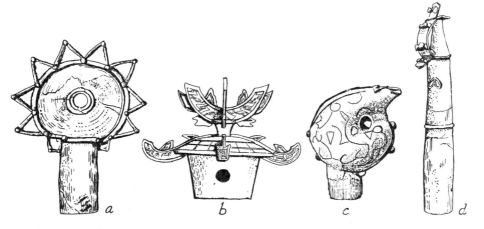

Fig. 58. Haniwa *fan, sunshade, archer's wrist-piece and sword: (a) Gumma, (b) Tomb of Hibasu-hime, Nara, (c) Isezaki city, Gumma, (d) Denenchōfu, Ōta ward, Tokyo, 40"*

Ise Shrine, where theoretically every twenty years the residence of the god is removed to a new sanctuary. In this ceremony, which follows closely a tenth-century book, *Engishiki,* certain symbols are traditionally carried: a long-handled umbrella, a fan with long handle, a spear, shield, quiver and sword. The sword is this *haniwa* type. The significance of such swords is therefore of a ceremonial nature seemingly unrelated to the cult of the dead and its requirements, but this does not preclude the possibility that these swords could have been carried in shrine and funerary processions, and transferred to shrine use only

Fig. 59

when government decree banned elaborate funerals, or that the noble to be interred had not been an individual of high rank in shrine affairs.

Glass from tombs is mostly in the form of beads, but a fine bowl, allegedly dug out of the tomb of Emperor Ankan (A.D. 534–5) in the Tokugawa era, and once owned by the Sairinji, is almost a mate to one from Emperor Nintoku's tomb. As neither can be Japanese in origin it would seem necessary to look even further than the continent in this case for possible sources, and perhaps to a place of manufacture in the Byzantine world. The earliest glass in Japan was discovered at Sugu and Mikumo in association with jar burials, and would date to the first century B.C. or A.D. These are complete or frag-mentary beads. Others of Yayoi times are known, including the *magatama* in glass. The *magatama*, however, could not have been made far afield, for only in Korea or Japan did it have any significance. It is possible that after the importation of raw materials from China (where a kind of lead glass was in use) glass was being locally made by the advent of the Tomb Period. One type from the sepulchres is an eye-catching variegated glass in imbedded circular colours, but it seems impossible that the technique of grinding and cutting could have reached a level sufficient to produce the Ankan and Nintoku bowls. Surely they represent contacts with distant countries on an emissarial level.

Local artisans were often quick to take up the reproduction of continental imports, but in the case of the mirrors a com-pletely foreign symbolism and the early obscure place the mirror had in the religious thinking may have acted as deterrents against their insular production. For three centuries Chinese trade met the Japanese demand, but when the supply started to dwindle due to the effects of the Buddhist religion on mirror making, the Japanese craftsmen were forced to take up the slack. This happened around the middle of the third century, and may be credited to the Yamato clique which, under the aegis of the Sun Goddess, was moving to strengthen its posi⁄tion, and the mirror, up to this time important only to the Kinki group as the solar symbol, became a sign of allegiance.

The prototype for most Japanese mirrors was the much⁄used platoon of Taoist divinities and animals, whose spirits had been given form in the Han Dynasty and whose representation persisted into Wei times with several variations. Infinite

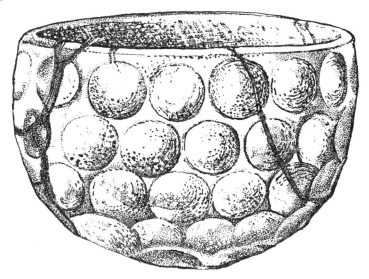

Fig. 59   Glass bowl traditionally from tomb of Emperor Ankan, Furuichi, Ōsaka. Height 3¼″

differences in Japan were based on units of three or four, and the subjects lost all marks of identification and receded into a realm of greater mystery in an amorphous and wormy state. Interesting instances may be pointed out where mirrors from the same mould are found together in a tomb, or even in tombs not too far distant, posing questions relating to the centres of production, control of distribution, and the presenting of mirrors as gifts, and signs of recognized authority.

Plate 91

To return to the Chinese ones briefly, one reference corresponding to A.D. 239 in the section on the people of Japan in the *Wei Chih* is concerned with the transmission of mirrors. The account states that Pei-mi-fu (Himeko in Japanese terminology, a standard term for a female ruler), the queen of Ya-ma-t'ai (Yamadai), gave the emperor of Wei many gifts and in return was sent a hundred bronze mirrors. The inaccuracies that accompany the story heighten the controversy over the location of Yamadai. The phonetic similarity to Yamato is quite obvious, and proponents of the Yamadai-equals-Yamato theory see confusion on the part of Wei writers who knew only West Japan well, and somehow identified a local ruler—a number of whom must have been female—with the highest Yamato sovereign. Those who hold the belief that Yamadai is in Kyūshū point out that no queen other than Empress Jingō ruled at the Yamato court, according to the annals. Empress Jingō's traditional dates would correspond favourably with this account, but her actual dates are 150 years later, and Wei chronology is more acceptable at this stage. The weight of evidence is on the side of those who equate Yamadai with the Yamato area, since many details of the Chinese description could apply only to a centre of substantial population such as that represented in the Kansai.

The Japanese mirrors frequently reached considerable size and were often profusely deposited in tombs. The mirror with four buildings was reputedly in the company of thirty-five others when removed in 1881. The Shinyama tomb contained twenty-three, including the three famous *chokkomon* mirrors. The two completely false inscription bands on one of the four TLV mirrors from this tomb is some affirmation that its contents are probably late fourth century or early fifth, and the TLV mirrors reproduce a little-understood and quite obsolete type. Totally startling inventions shine through the milieu of continental derivations by the fifth century, however, and the

Plate 90

Plate 88

most surprising and characteristically Japanese at this stage is the one from Gumma bearing men carrying swords and shields. Unfortunately this and the mirror with buildings are ancient discoveries without documentation; nevertheless, the latter at least has a very genuine appearance, even preserving some of the textile in which it was wrapped. Less positive statements can be made for the one with hunting figures. Its enamel-green finish is unusual, and its decoration confused. It will be noticed that the men are all left-handed, hold an oddly-shaped shield in the right hand, and although the mirror is traditionally referred to as a 'hunting design mirror', the hunters have no interest whatever in the deer. Shields would seem to be a useless burden for such a chase—or even for a dance preparatory to a hunt of animals no more vicious than deer. The little men stand with legs apart, frontally represented, their frog-like feet in profile; the brandished swords look suspiciously double-edged. The total effect is one of a stereotyped dance. Space-filling circles and parallel lines, and separating bars and knobs provide pig-tails in a number of cases, and at one place in the inner circle a jar with flared mouth may be seen. Obviously there were no races of left-handers or one could trust the Chinese writers to have mentioned them, and the caster simply did not follow through with his design and get it reversed for a correct picture. One still falls back on the idea of a ritual dance with magical import before setting forth on the chase, but this explanation seems thin. All things considered, however, its farcical treatment of almost credible subject-matter can hardly be simply explained away as incompetence on the part of the maker.

Plate 92

Almost sixty jingle-bell mirrors with known provenance stand as graphic demonstration of how continental objects were accepted and transformed by the native stamp. In analysing the discoveries, Morimoto found that the great majority are from the central mountains; the Kantō and Tōkai follow, and

Plate 87

then the Yamato region. They are rare through the Inland Sea and two are reported from Kyūshū, and bells on bracelets, incidentally, adhere closely to the same distribution. Also, most have five bells, but the number is usually proportional to the size of the mirror and may result in both even and odd numbers.[30] The mirror itself was indiscriminately selected, any current design and an occasional Chinese one being satisfactory. On the whole, while spanning the militant Middle Tomb phase and the Late, these form a part of the culture of the horse-riding gentry of the first half of the Late period, although their distribution is not exactly co-ordinated with horse trappings.

The domestic pottery of the Tomb period receives its name from the ancient records in which *Haji* was the descriptive title given to clay workers. The Hajibe was thus the guild of potters. Since Haji pottery seems to have been required in far smaller lots than the Sue, the other protohistoric type, and was also more native in tradition, it does not have the commercialized and mass-produced look that characterizes the ceremonial Sue. *Fig. 60* Haji is red pottery, following in the direct family line of Yayoi, is normally undecorated and fashioned in rather limited shapes, the majority of which are round bottomed. Surface scratching was occasionally employed, and in a unique example, which may show that even Haji could have some *Fig. 60f* ceremonial use, a human-headed vessel was discovered under stones in circumstances that had all the indications of a deliberate deposit. Rice husks were still preserved within, and its outer surface bears a coating of red paint.

It is difficult to know exactly where and when Yayoi was transformed into Haji, but probably in the Kinki, and most likely at the time its makers were organized and appointed by regions. Early Haji is by no means easily separated from Late Yayoi, and is distinguished chiefly on the basis of loss of decoration and change in shape. Haji reached its peak of production during the fifth century, and lasted at least as long as the eighth, by which time it had pushed north even into South Hokkaidō. Local names are frequently given for regions, the most common one in use being Izumi for the Kantō area.

The Hajibe were designated caretakers of tombs in the time of Emperor Suinin when they assumed the duty of making the clay sculptures (*haniwa*) for the mounds. The literature only verifies what is evident in the archaeological situation—that the *haniwa* and Haji have a common ancestry. This means, therefore, that pottery for the exterior of the tomb was the work of one guild, for the interior (Sue) another, an interesting division of labour that is explained by the development of two distinct

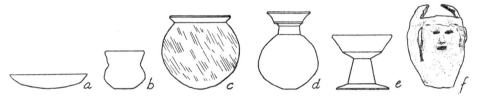

Fig. 60   Haji pottery: (a) Suwada, Ichikawa city, Chiba, (b) Miike, Shizuoka, (c) Furudome, Nara, (d) Chausuyama tomb, Sakurai, Nara, (e) Ishitsu, Ōsaka, (f) Hoshina, Nagano. Height of (f) 5⅛", others to scale

traditions. Another book, the *Engishiki*, names three kinds: Haji, Sue and Shino, each made by guilds.

The Sue (or *Iwaibe*, 'ceremonial ware', now considered to be an incorrect usage) is the funerary pottery that was introduced by Koreans and produced in shops of a highly trained guild that must have been Korean at the core. The assumption has been that Sue arrived at the time Emperor Yūriaku was on the throne in the midfifth century, and in the year corresponding to A.D. 473 this ruler ordered the guild to fashion vessels suitable for his morning and evening meals, which potters from Settsu, Yamashiro, Ise, Tamba, Tajima and Inaba (provinces of the Kinki and near by) were to supply. This is none other than a list of centres of manufacture, and there are other indications that it was made in Bizen, Harima and Ōwari of the Inland Sea and southern Tōkai. It may have actually appeared in the Kinki in the latter part of the fourth or fifth century, but it flourished excessively in the sixth century and survived well into the Buddhist era, for it has now been shown that some kilns did double duty in furnishing vessels for tombs and tiles for temple roofs.

Whereas often Haji is classified as strictly domestic and Sue as ceremonial, it may be more exact to say that the former was for use by the masses, and the latter was upper-class ware, except perhaps in West Japan where Sue is so plentiful it could hardly have been limited to the aristocracy only. It is the tombs which draw the line between the classes, and thus show the distinction in pottery by their contents. An occasional community site has some Sue in its litter; it is in pits of dwellings in the Kantō, and even more frequent in the Kansai where living standards were higher. Also, as pointed out above, Haji can even have a ceremonial use at times, and the dividing lines may not be as sharp as archaeologists would like to believe.

The incredible quantity of Sue ware has been subjected to regional and temporal classifications, but it has an amazing homogeneity as a consequence of the uniformity of training of potters and perfected controls of the techniques. In general terms it is a grey pottery, varying from brown through bluish-grey to almost black, often lighter clay at the core than on the surface. It is thin, light in weight, rather brittle, obviously fired at a high temperature. In some cases a salty glaze has appeared as a result of extreme heat, but the influence of continental practices in glazing is not readily recognizable until around the seventh century. As pottery made on a fast wheel, the fine rings are scrupulously preserved, and may be the only surface effect. When decoration is used, the customary manner is a combing in bands of lines, often zigzag. One may also see a surviving cord-marking, or check-stamps produced with the aid of a paddle.

Fig. 61   Pottery steamer from Sanjō tomb, Ashiya city, Hyōgo. Height about 11" when assembled

The question of the extent to which Sue was in daily use by upper classes cannot be answered, but a domestic object in constant demand was the three-unit cooking stove, several of which have been recovered from tombs in the Kinki region. The uppermost bowl with lugs is a strainer with five or more holes in its floor, but frequently the holes are far too large for anything the size of rice grains, implying that in the case of the

Fig. 61

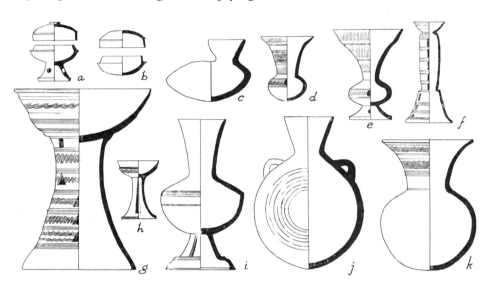

Fig. 62   Sue pottery: (a) Ōtsukayama tomb, Hyōgo, (b) Sakai, Ōsaka, (c, i) Ōyabu tomb, Osaka, (d, g, h, k) Inariyama tomb, Shiga, (e, j), Kinrei tomb, Chiba, (f) Tsushima, Nagasaki. Height of (g) 24", others to scale

stoves destined for the tombs, function was no object. Some have a fourth piece, an upright cylinder on which the strainer can be set after removal from the other sections.

Tall and short cups on pedestals, the smaller ones with lids, are exceedingly numerous. Perforations in the stems of the larger libation vessels are triangular, rectangular or at times circular in shape, and may be seen in the Korean antecedents.

Fig. 62

Other vessels with globular bodies normally have trumpet-shaped necks and mouths. A few unexpected shapes break the monotony, but on the whole, manufacture continued with deadly regularity, guided by the mass-production principle.

Larger vases, usually on tall stands and supplied with a number of shoulder cups, sometimes carry grotesque groups of human and animal figures, and occasionally other subjects, all quite Sillan in idea. The feeble articulation of many of the little sculptures is a drawback to adequate identification, but as they belong to mortuary libation vessels, the subjects by and large should have to do with funerary activities including entertainment, animal sacrifices, and transportation of the spirit of the dead. The Inland Sea zone merges with the Kinki to yield the

Plate 95   finest examples. One of the largest from Okayama would appear to have a pair of wrestlers, another individual who in modern terminology might be the referee, a horse, and a man on horseback. A less complete vase, whose provenance is

Plate 94   probably also this same area, carries a boat containing four men, three of whom pull on oars while the other handles a broader oar at the stern. The unillustrated side bears animals that are a stag with two does and a badly damaged animal, perhaps a fourth deer, and two more creatures, possibly a boar and dog. Although of considerable interest, obviously the makers of these had lost certain skills demonstrated by their Silla predecessors, and had not developed the experience the Haji makers had in their production of the tomb *haniwa*.

THE TOMB SCULPTURES

To avoid using unwieldly phrases that mean sculptures placed on the slopes of tombs, I have employed the Japanese term *haniwa*. Literally this should signify a clay circle, and by application would be a clay cylinder, but because they were at various times arranged in the shape of a ring, there may be some connection in the terminology with their placement. The origin of the term is described in the *Nihon Shoki* in connection with a story that purports to explain the beginnings of the practice. It came about during the reign of Emperor Suinin (third century A.D. probably) when on the death of his uncle '. . . his personal attendants were assembled, and were all buried alive upright in the precinct of the *misasagi*. For several days they died not, but wept and wailed day and night. At last they died and rotted. Dogs and crows gathered and ate them.'[31] Horrified, as if this were his first unpleasant experience with the custom, the emperor suggested counsel be taken so as to put a stop to the practice. The *Kojiki* actually says this is the first time it happened, but the full *Nihon Shoki* account implies it was a rather ancient custom. When the empress died some five years later, the opportunity came. Nomi-no-Sukune, a famous wrestler, proposed to send to Izumo and get a hundred men of the clay workers' guild and have them make substitutes for men, horses and others things to be set up at the mound. All of this was done; they were first placed on the tomb of Hibasu-hime-no-Mikoto, and the name given to these clay objects was *haniwa*. The emperor was most grateful, Nomi-no-Sukune was rewarded, and given a 'kneading place' and appointed official in charge of the clay workers' guild. His name was changed to Haji-no-Omi, and the account closes by saying that this is how it happened that the Haji-no-Omi superintend the burials of the emperors.

Archaeologists have yet to demonstrate that this graphic story of the origins of the sculptures has any basis in fact. Burial alive or immolation have been proved to have existed in China, but it would not have taken place within the tomb in Japan or in circumstances that would provide the least kind of preservation for the remains, and as logical as the practice might have been in conditions of virtual slavery and absolute rule, it was probably not very widespread. For those who are looking for corroboration of the story, it is a pleasant thought to know that *haniwa* have been found in recent years on the tomb that the *Nihon Shoki* appears to specify as that built for the wife of Emperor Suinin. If this traditional explanation is not accepted, the difficulties in seeing the sculptures arise under foreign influence are even greater, merely because they lack any similarity to the continental tomb figurines, where amongst other differences, they were deposited inside the tomb. It is clear that the origins story is an attempt to rationalize this difference, and to show why they stand outside the tombs, pressed into the ground. The native character of these, however, is deeply imbedded in a rather long tradition—first appearing with Yayoi potters, then the succeeding Haji, and carried into their further assignment to make images for the mounds. Apparently those in charge of tomb maintenance still perpetuated the legend of the origins, and so it entered the literature, although *haniwa* had been obsolete for approximately two centuries. If tomb care was what it should have been, the *haniwa* could still be seen standing on the mounds when the annals were committed to writing.

The density of *haniwa* in the Yamato area would bear on this matter of origin. They are rather rare in Kyūshū, where a maritime culture demonstrated an interest in boats, and where many *haniwa* are obviously modelled after Kansai types. Similarly they are not common in the Izumo area, from whence the first potters were supposed to have come. The Okayama region has quite a few, though largely provincial in nature, but the tombs of the Kantō, into the Gumma lower mountains of the north-west, and southern Tōhoku in the north are liberally sprinkled with figures, particularly of animals and men. The development reaches its maximum in this area, the primitive tradition evolving unhampered toward a logical fruition, whereas in the Kinki the expanding pressures

Plate 102

that erupted in the Buddhist culture cut the development pre-
maturely. Horses and symbolic objects, on the whole slightly
earlier, are particularly well portrayed in the Yamato region.

In very general terms the inanimate objects antedate the
human beings, and are chiefly of the fifth rather than the sixth
century; in fact, some seem to have appeared even before that.

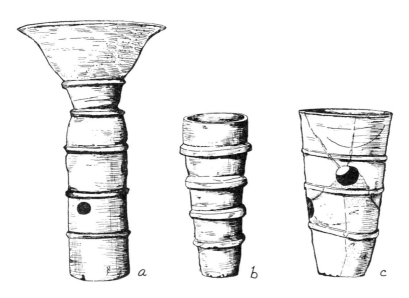

Fig. 63   Haniwa *cylinders from tombs:* (a) *uncertain,* (b) *Higashiyama, Aichi,*
about 17½″, (c) *Miyake, Nara*

The earliest of any sort are the cylinders, of perhaps the late
third century, and they may be found wherever the tombs were
constructed. The origins story in the literature, incidentally,
does not take into consideration the fact that the cylinders precede the images by about a century, a fact probably quite
unknown to the recorders. These cylinders were lined up on
the tomb banks like terraces, even in triple file, often arranged
circularly or cutting sharp angles along the square front of a

Fig. 63

Fig. 63a

tumulus. Early ones were widely spaced, but by the fifth century they were standing side-by-side. They were also staggered, zigzag in effect. A few have a 'morning glory' top, and were sometimes used as accents in rows of the simpler kind. As to position they may be only at the top, only at the bottom, or elsewhere, and along with the fact that earlier ones are frequently 6 feet apart, these factors would seem to dilute the theory that they were invented to prevent erosion of the slopes. Other suggestions are that they were decorative in intent; or they were phallic in design. Gotō believes that they formed a protective barrier or symbolic fence that marks the precincts of the tomb.[32] If so, the three moats and 20,000 cylinders guarding Emperor Nintoku's grave must have constituted a formidable cordon, most discouraging to malevolent spirits. It is unnecessary to add that had this tomb been a twentieth-century public works project, it could hardly have been conceived and carried out on a more gigantic scale.

It is not hard to see that by adding a few physical details the development could readily progress to the cylindrically shaped figures which compose a high per cent of the *haniwa* images. Some are little more than an extended tube with abbreviated human features, while later ones are products of increasing articulation in modelling that brings out the forms more realistically. It is the naïve simplicity and cubistic character that catches the eye of the modern observer, attuned to abstraction and primitivisms in contemporary sculpture.

Plate 99

The offering bearers, entertainers, dancers, comedians, both male and female, were participants in the ceremonies during the period of mourning. The musicians—*koto* (harp) players, drum beaters, and others—wear special costumes; deeply kowtowing figures may have been reciters, and make one think of a prototype for the Kabuki actor. Men in armour usually stood on the top and often at the front of the tomb, and while representing the warriors of the funeral procession also took

their posts as tomb guards. In full regalia the best of these give
a remarkable picture of the well-equipped military man. He
wears his leather armour tied across, left over right, while his
daily costume is fastened the opposite way. Quivers on the
back are probably in place for ceremonial occasions, on the
side for actual combat.

Plate 96

Men in general are more frequently portrayed than women,
and the latter includes a group that is loosely referred to as
mediums, who must have played a part in the religious affairs
of early Shintō. Long-robed individuals largely belong to the
nobility stratum, whereas half-length figures are often in more
sketchy treatment and represent a servant class. In keeping with
the lower position of women in society, the half-length figure
is the most common in that sex. Unquestionably, a large group
of women presided at the funeral ceremonies—a woman's job.
In regard to the lower classes, the aristocratic looking figure
who has a curved sickle at the waist and quite rarely a hoe on
one shoulder, resembles more an estate owner than just the
farm hand. In coolie hat, he may even wear ear-rings.

The female figures are clothed in a jacket with tight-fitting
collar, narrow sleeves and slightly flared skirt. They wear ear
and neck jewellery, hair combs over the forehead, and often a
flat hat like a mortar-board. The *magatama* necklace enjoyed
considerable popularity with the ladies. The usual hair arrangement for unmarried girls was long and hanging over the neck;
for married women it was shorter, and men parted their hair
in the middle, separating it like truncated pigtails to dangle
across the ears to the shoulders. Jewellery for men was also
fashionable, and men's hats were designed in all imaginable
varieties, some undoubtedly with special significance conform-
ing to the occupation of the wearer.

Plate 98

Plate 97

Many of the faces have been touched up with paint, usually
extending from the eyes, sometimes in full coverage, or just on
the forehead, and occasionally down over the neck. There is no

Fig. 64a–f

Fig. 64 Haniwa *heads illustrating hats and face painting:* (a) *Minowa, Gumma,* (b) *Yoshimi,* (g) *Ibaragi,* (h) *uncertain,* (i) *Ōkawa, Gumma,* (j) *Tega, Chiba,* (k) *Akitsu, Ibaragi,*

distinction between male and female, military and civilian, entertainer or otherwise. It probably represents a common

*Saitama, (c) Minami-tachibana, Gumma, (d) Takami, Fukushima, (e) Tatsukawa, Tochigi, (f) Gumma,
(l) Misato, Gumma*

practice of beautification and not tattooing, although tattooing
at the time of Emperor Richū was in use by a number of tribes,

199

but it was most likely done in black soot. The Chinese accounts mention that tattooing was practised in Japan in a record that reads chiefly like an inventory of customs considered to be barbaric. Later face tattooing was in effect branding, a punishment for offences. It should be added that painting of other parts of the *haniwa* in a red colour is by no means unusual, and headgear, costumes, or arms and armour may all bear it.

Plates 100, 101

The animals, too, were sunken into the ground for a secure stance, and when one sees them today out of context the legs appear inordinately large. Be that as it may, the friendliness of the dogs, the intelligence of the horses, the sinister character of the boars, or timid look of the deer are all strangely but pleasantly expressed in simply modelled surfaces, eyes and mouths rarely more than punctures. Through the use of smooth transitions the ultimate contrasts between the deep shadows and strong highlights sharpen the sensation of latent vitality. Horses are the most familiar, chickens next, then deer, boar, dogs and a rare monkey and rabbit. Had this been Yayoi times the animals of food value would have appeared most often, but the relative frequence of subjects obviously indicates they take a secondary position. The horse has already been discussed as the animal on which the nobles depended to maintain their position, but the barnyard fowl can only be explained in terms of something like the story of the Sun Goddess seeking refuge in a cavern after her brother had made himself utterly detestable, and taking the light of day with her. Three inducements eventually lured her out: dancing, a cock crowing, and the sight of her own reflection in a mirror. The cock had become a symbol of a vague hope for the dead—as exemplified in the resurrection of the Sun Goddess, and its crowing must have been one of the preferred sounds at funerals, as Gotō indicates.[33]

One final word in connection with stone figures that were designed either for tombs, or are a carryover from the pre

Buddhist primitive treatment into the Buddhist period. Over a dozen tomb sites in Kyūshū (Fukuoka, Kumamoto, Ōita prefectures) have or had stone figures, and of all the sites, the Sekijinyama (Stone Men Mountain) tomb has the most famous. These include horses, now usually fragmentary, at least lacking legs. Quite typical in these sculptures is the quiver which when seen from the front shows the inset head of a man at the top. Besides this, there are simplified figures in armour, heads in completely abstract form. Three feet is the average height, and they are either rectangular or cylindrical in cross-section.

In the Kansai a number of images have been transported from fields of the old Asuka area to tombs, and in certain cases to museum grounds. Twice moved and now sitting along the front of a small tomb near the great mound of Emperor Kaimei are four odd stone figures, two of which are male, two female. Plates 107, 108 These look so much like apes they have been nicknamed *saruseki* (monkey stones). The female figures at least are traditionally deities of childbirth, and although they may be early Buddhist in time, I include them because I believe they personify and perpetuate pre-Buddhist native concepts, but of course fashioned in an earthy and subhuman way that clearly speaks against any history of stone carving in the area. The refined and rather sophisticated Kyūshū figures, on the other hand, are evidence of certain accomplishments that might be explained once again by the nearness of the region to a ready source of skilled craftsmen.

THE SHRINES

In its early form Shintō was a vague belief in a multitude of natural spirits, particularly those which resided in shaded groves, on mountain tops, near water sources, around unusual stones, and virtually everywhere in the picturesque landscape. Needless to say, concepts and accompanying practices went through some evolution, regardless of the level at which they were later to be maintained: the fear which dominated the Neo-lithic period changed to a more relaxed and optimistic attitude in Yayoi times, and symbols that had had a personal meaning were transferred to group use in the atmosphere of progressing community co-operation. The gods were fully benign by the protohistoric era, and served the emperor and people well; they became the object of sacrifices and thank-offerings, and were credited with good taste in their choice of verdant and exotic sites for residence. Religious ceremonies included ablutions and cleansing to avoid pollution by unclean matter, and therefore the involvement with the unclean dead and funeral rituals came under the jurisdiction of liturgists, diviners, and other figures of a sacerdotal nature.

The sun and moon had by this time assumed a firm position in the pantheon, and the worship of Amaterasu, the Sun Goddess, may have started in the protohistoric era within the imperial family, permeated the clan, and branched out to be an accepted practice amongst all loyal Iron Age kingdoms. Thus the pact between the Izumo and Yamato gods to give the former charge over religious affairs and the latter control of political matters was in effect nullified—a foregone conclusion —unless one considers that compensation took the form of putting the tombs in custody of Izumo men and so retaining for them a religious trade. Anyway, the political value of the banner of the Sun Goddess was early recognized, but the final *coup* that forced the institutionalization of Shintō was the competitive force of the fully evolved concepts of Buddhism that threatened to swamp primitive and unsocial animism. The vast and loose host of gods had little relation to each other, and without inquiry into their nature and the meaning of life, no real philosophy could be expected to develop. Quite obviously the deities were not sufficiently personal or in sharp enough focus to have been represented graphically, and even after centuries of Buddhist image-making, Shintō deities were still only rarely portrayed—an indication that as spirits of nature there was no way they could be effectively translated into human form. Its title, *Shintō*, meaning 'the Way of the Gods', was applied only a few years after Buddhism appeared, and is a term that suggests inspiration from Chinese Taoist sources.

The early symbols of the sword, *magatama* and mirror had their beginnings in prehistoric periods, but other typical features of shrines and their activities also had a very ancient history, and probably date to long before the religion was even graced by a title: the *torii*, the sacred gate at the entrance of every shrine and often repeated, was the bird perch on which the cock sat while crowing for the Sun Goddess to come forth from the cavern; the straw rope tied to the *torii* kept the goddess from re-entering the cave; the inducement dance that drew her out is still practised. Certain features that have crept into Shintō in later times have been rigorously purged in order to purify it and recover its original (or protohistoric) character.

There is no reason to believe that shrines were not built before Buddhism suggested the idea of providing a house for the god. A box-like shelter modelled after a dwelling was constructed, where a symbol could be deposited, or left empty as a place for divine residence. Since the god had numerous counterparts serving other needs, buildings at shrines multiplied in similar form or as miniature receptacles in the compound. The great Izumo Shrine is traditionally representative of the god-house being patterned after the dwelling since the shrine is dedicated to Ōkuni-nushi-no-Mikoto, the father of fishing, medicine and sericulture, who retired in the region of his sovereignty and for whom a palace was built. Thus the earliest shrine type is traditionally an upper class dwelling, raised on a platform. Situated on the north coast of Chūgoku in Shimane

Plate 104

Fig. 65a

Fig. 65b, c

Plate 105

prefecture, the shrine is the oldest of all in terms of its plan. The *Nihon Shoki* specifies a large building in the account of its founding, but even though the main structure has been reduced in subsequent reconstructions, it is still of impressive magnitude. The compound is necessarily capacious because it is the gathering place of all the deities during the month of October each year (and Shintō had eight million by an early census), in a process that suggests the rejuvenation concept which is dramatized in the rebuilding of Ise Shrine every twenty years. Although Izumo has picked up Chinese features in its rectangular precinct and balconied buildings, and lost its obvious primitivity in the placement of the roof members, internally its arrangement with a central pillar and entrance off-centre on a short side means the deity enjoys full privacy behind a partition in the same way Yayoi people might have in their raised dwellings. The supporting posts for the ridge-pole took the blame for the off-centre entrance, and their presence has already been pointed out on the Yayoi bronze bell and at the Ise Shrine, but they were dispensed with by protohistoric times. Izumo is therefore Yayoi in character.

Two shrines a few miles south of Ōsaka were built without evidence of this pole: Ōtori and Sumiyoshi. There the doorway is located in the middle at one end of the long axis, the centre-post discarded. Sumiyoshi is on human scale, but in its red and white paint, it is out of keeping with the earnest attempts to retain the primitive look that the rebuilding in simple wood effects and roofing in cypress bark (replacing ancient reeds) has been able to do at other shrines. The Sumiyoshi shrines are actually four in number, three in line and one to the side—as if the fourth counts cadence for the others—and the closely spaced fences for each building hold off the worshipper or visitor at only arm's length compared with the remote distances at others. The four are dedicated to three offspring of Izanagi and Izanami, and one more deity, three of which are protectors

IZUMO ŌTORI SUMIYOSHI ISE

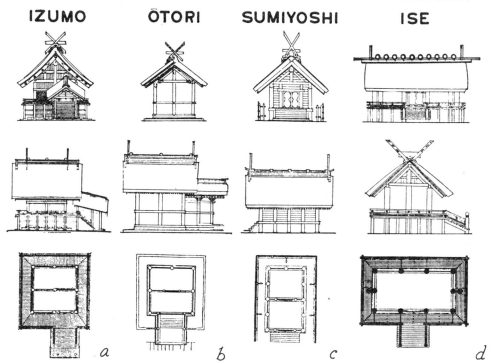

*Fig. 65 Diagrams of ancient shrine types still in use: (a) Izumo, Shimane, (b) Ōtori, Ōsaka,
(c) Sumiyoshi, Ōsaka, (d) Ise, Mie*

of seafarers. The shrine is no longer beside the water because of a
two-mile reclamation of land, but this seems not to have been
instrumental in any way in moulding the developing belief
that its gods are also the patron saints of rice-wine drinkers.
The origins of this shrine are obscured in early history, although
one legend lists its founding by Empress Jingō, but possibly
an eighth-century date is most suitable. It was apparently once
involved in the twenty-year rebuilding plan, but the last took
place around A.D. 1221, and the present structures were largely
reconditioned in 1862.

The Ōtori shrine is not on a platform, but the raised system is employed in all the other primitive types. Of the four, Ōtori is the least distinguished, though hardly for this reason. One tradition claims establishment during the reign of Emperor Suinin, and the Fujiwara family had a special attachment to it since its members were descended from the god enshrined within, Ama-no-koyane-no-Mikoto, a reciter of poetry whose fame lay in the fact that he hung the mirror on the tree that lured the Sun Goddess from the cave. The lack of a balcony and almost square shape are among its pedestrian features, and technically speaking, as a type it precedes Sumiyoshi.

Fig. 65d

The most sacred of all is Ise at Uji-Yamada on the east side of the Kii Peninsula where the mirror of the solar deity is preserved. The Inner and Outer Shrines, two almost identical precincts four miles apart, have been too hallowed to be changed, or to be reproduced in illustrations until recent years. The Inner Shrine was founded by the energetic Suinin as the sacred habitation of Amaterasu-no-Ōmikami; the Outer Shrine, near the railway station, is dedicated to Toyouke-no-Ōmikami, goddess of agriculture and sericulture, and is believed to have once been a shrine in Kyōto that was moved to this spot by Emperor Yūriaku in A.D. 478. In a setting of Japanese cedar trees of incredible beauty, the shrines are theoretically reconstructed every two decades on adjoining lots. In earlier times and due to the war this has not always been possible, but the fifty-ninth rebuilding since the inauguration of the practice in the seventh century was carried out in 1954. The cypress-wood colours are preserved throughout except for gold tips on roof members, the buildings constructed without nails or benefit of complicated joints. Paradoxically these shrines are the most primitive structurally yet the most advanced organizationally of all the pre-Buddhistic types still in use today.

At both shrines four wooden palings surround a group of buildings that are oriented to the south and have their entrances on the long side. As if approaching a Forbidden and Inner City where the palace stands at the north end, and not unlike some ideas used at Naniwa, the ancient Ōsaka, the worshipper passes a spirit screen on the south and enters only the first *torii*. From there he can see through the layers of heightening sanctity to the holy of holies which sits on a platform near the middle of the innermost rectangle. As the rectangles are related in such an eccentric way that considerable space separates the fences which stand between the worshipper and shrine proper (but not at the back), the main building is actually at the north end of the precinct. Smaller structures of the same design as the chief shrine are placed to right and left, somewhat to the front in the Outer Shrine, and to the back in the case of the Inner Shrine. While an inability to penetrate beyond the worship altar of the second fence may frustrate a none-too-ardent Shintōist, identical buildings on a lesser scale are scattered through the open grounds and may be inspected closely.

Plate 106

The casual observer might not be aware of the other paradoxes that make Ise a cross-section of Japan in any of the many centuries that the borders of the country have been open, and the people sensitive and receptive to innovations from the continent. Ise is Japanese to the core, yet the dualism of the shrines and numerous other continental aspects are prominent —in some ways even dominant—but are neatly integrated with the surroundings and synthesized to suit the simplicity and tranquillity of the atmosphere. This talent for harmonizing the introductions with established native practices was exercised during a half millennium of pre-Buddhist centuries; Ise summarizes it and exhibits it at its best.

Text References

Where details of publications are not given, see Bibliography

1 See J. Maringer, 'A Core and Flake Industry of Palaeolithic Type from Central Japan'.

2 S. Sugihara in section on Old Stone Age in *An Illustrated Cultural History of Japan*, 1, 84.

3 S. Yamanouchi, 'The Main Divisions and Subdivisions of Jōmon Pottery', 1937.

4 G. J. Groot, *The Prehistory of Japan*, 6ff.

5 See J. E. Kidder, Jr., *The Jōmon Pottery of Japan*, 15–16.

6 K. Ōyama, 'The Chronology of the Jōmon Culture of the Stone Age in the Kantō', or 'Vorläufiger Bericht über die Chronologie der Jōmon-Kultur der Steinzeit im Kantō'.

7 See N. Sakazume, 'Shell-mounds in the Kantō and Their Pottery'.

8 N. G. Munro, *Prehistoric Japan*, 54–5.

9 *Op. cit.*, 53.

10 *Op. cit.*, 150.

11 K. Kindaichi, 'The Theory that the Ainu were Ezo'.

12 See Y. Imamura and Z. Ikeda, 'Dr. Kiyono's Theory of the Japanese Race'.

13 Mori demonstrated that this generally believed development is actually true. See 'Archaeological Study of Jar-Burials in Eneolithic Japan'.

14 Translated by W. G. Aston, *Nihongi*, 1, 215–16.

15 J. Buhot, *Histoire des Arts du Japon*, 33–4.

16 S. Sugihara in section on Yayoi pottery in *An Illustrated Cultural History of Japan*, 1, 183–4.

17 *Nihongi*, 1, 277.

18 *Op. cit.*, 280.

19 *Op. cit.*, 112.

20 Translated by B. H. Chamberlain, *Kojiki*, 389.

21 M. Suenaga, *Old Tombs from the Air*, 3, 13.

22 Buhot, *op. cit.*, 270.

23 Suenaga, *op. cit.*, 36–7.

24 *Nihongi*, 1, 326.

25 *Nihongi*, 11, 218–19.

26 See E. Ishida, M. Oka, N. Egami and I. Yawata, *Origin of the Japanese People*, 139–53; see also R. K. Beardsley, 'Japan Before History', 341–2.

27 R. Morimoto, *Studies in Japanese Archaeology*, 414–30.

28 K. Hamada and S. Umehara, 'Ancient Tomb at Mizuo', English section, 17–18.

29 S. Gotō, *Study of the Ancient Japanese Culture*, 109–42.

30 Morimoto, *op. cit.*, 432–70.

31 *Nihongi*, 1, 178.

32 Gotō, *op. cit.*, 90–1.

Emperors preceding the introduction of Buddhism

	Traditional dates of reign	Age in Kojiki	Age in Nihon Shoki	Reign length in K and N S	Approximate adjusted dates
JIMMU	660–585 B.C.	137	127		1st c. B.C.–1st c. A.D.
SUIZEI	581–549	45	80		1st c. A.D.
ANNEI	548–511	49	57		1st c.
ITOKU	510–477	45	77		1st c.
KŌSHŌ	475–393	93	113		1st c.
KŌAN	392–291	123		N S 102	2nd c.
KŌREI	290–215	106		N S 76	2nd c.
KŌKEN	214–158	57		N S 57	2nd c.
KAIKA	157–98	63		N S 60	3rd c.
SŪJIN	97–30	168	120		219–249
SUININ	29 B.C.– A.D. 70	153	140		249–280
KEIKŌ	71–130	137	106		280–316
SEIMU	131–190	95	107		316–343
CHŪAI	191–200	52	52		343–346
⌠ JINGŌ ⎨ (empress)	201–269	100	100		
⌡ ŌJIN	270–310	130	110		346–395
NINTOKU	313–399	83		N S 87	395–427
RICHŪ	400–405	64	70		427–432
HANZEI	406–411	60		N S 6	433–438
INGYŌ	412–453	78		N S 42	438–453
ANKŌ	454–456	56		N S 3	
YŪRIAKU	457–479	124		N S 23	
SEINEI	480–484			N S 5	
KENZŌ	485–487	38		N S 3	
NINKEN	488–498			N S 11	
MURETSU	499–506			N S 8; K 8	
KEITAI	507–531	43	82		
ANKAN	534–535		70		
SENKUWA	536–539		73		
KIMMEI	540–571			N S 32	

Short Bibliography

It would be unfair not to give credit where it is due in regard to the chief sources I have utilized, although in a selected bibliography it is only token credit and may appear in an arbitrary light. A survey of Japanese pre-history cannot possibly be drawn from sources in western languages, and the reader is cautioned in his use of reference materials antedating the mid-thirties. The bulk of the bibliography may be found in Japanese in the following and a host of other periodicals, a very few of which have English summaries: *Dorumen* (Dolmen), 1932–5, 4 vols.; *Dōtaku* (Bronze Bell), 1932–; *Jinruigaku Senshigaku Kōza* (Symposium on Anthropology and Prehistory), 1938–41, 19 vols.; *Jinruigaku Zasshi* (Journal of Anthropology), 1886–; *Kaizuka* (Shell-mound), 1938–; *Kodai* (Ancient Culture) 1951–; *Kodaigaku* (Studies in Ancient Culture), 1952–; *Kodaigaku Kenkyū* (Studies in Antiquity), 1949–; *Kōkogaku* (Archaeology), 1930–41; *Kōkogaku Nempō* (Annual of Archaeology), 1948–; *Kōkogaku Zasshi* (Journal of Archaeology), 1910–; *Kyōto Teikoku Daigaku Kōkogaku Kenkyū Hōkoku* (Reports of Archaeological Research, Kyōto Imperial University), 1917–43, 16 vols.; *Sekki Jidai* (Stone Age), 1955–; *Senshi-kōkogaku* (Prehistoric Archaeology), 1937, 1 vol.; *Shizengaku Zasshi* (Journal of Prehistory), 1929–43, 15 vols.

The Japanese bibliography is written entirely in English since trans-literation consumes too much space, but the reader will find summaries in English where the notation is marked with an asterisk (*), in German if indicated by a dagger (†). The following abbreviations are used:

J G Z   *Jinruigaku Zasshi* (Journal of Anthropology)

J R G K   *Jinruigaku Senshigaku Kōza* (Symposium on Anthropology and Prehistory)

K G Z   *Kōkogaku Zasshi* (Journal of Archaeology)

K K   *Kobunkazai no Kagaku* (Scientific Papers on Antiques)

K T D K H   *Kyōto Teikoku Daigaku Kōkogaku Kenkyū Hōkoku* (Reports of Archaeological Research, Kyōto Imperial University)

MGK	*Minzokugaku Kenkyū* (Studies in Ethnology)
NM	*Nihon Minzoku* (Japanese Ethnology)
SJ	*Sekki Jidai* (Stone Age)
SKG	*Senshikōkogaku* (Prehistoric Archaeology)
SGZ	*Shizengaku Zasshi* (Journal of Prehistory)

Books and Articles in Japanese

COMMISSION FOR THE PROTECTION OF CULTURAL PROPERTIES, *The Shell Mounds of Yoshigo*, Tokyo, 1952*; *The Stone Remains of Ōyumachi*, Tokyo, 1953*; *The Dolmens at Shito*, Tokyo, 1956.*

ESAKA, T., *Jōmon Culture* (Prehistoric Periods, II), Tokyo, 1957.

GOTŌ, S., *The Chausuyama Tomb at Imai, Akabori Village, Sawa County, Kozuke*, Tokyo, 1932*; 'Dwellings in Ancient Times,' *JRGK*, XV, 1940, pp. 1–79; XVI, 1941, pp. 80–156; XVII, 1941, pp. 157–208; *Study of the Ancient Japanese Culture*, Tokyo, 1942; (general editor) *Toro: A Report on the Excavations of the Toro Sites*, (1948–50), Tokyo, 1954.*

HAMADA, K., 'Report on the Excavation of a Neolithic Site at Kō in the Province of Kawachi', *KTDKH*, II, 1918*; 'A Second Excavation at Kō, a Neolithic Site in the Province of Kawachi', *KTDKH*, IV, 1920*; 'The Megalithic Tomb Ishibutai at Shimanoshō in the Province of Yamato', *KTDKH*, XIV, 1937.*

HAMADA, K., AND UMEHARA, S., 'Ornamented Tombs in the Province of Higo', *KTDKH*, I, 1917; 'Ancient Tomb at Mizuo, Takashima County, in the Province of Omi', *KTDKH*, VIII, 1923.*

HAMADA, K., UMEHARA, S., AND SHIMADA, S., 'Ornamented Tombs in the Island of Kyūshū', *KTDKH*, III, 1919.*

HASEBE, K., 'The Existence of Cattle Breeding during the Stone Age', *JGZ*, LIV/10, 1939, pp. 447–50; 'On the Cranium of a Cat from the Nojima Shell-mound in the Early Jōmon Period', *JGZ*, LXV/7, 1956, pp. 128–34.*

HAYASHIDA, S., 'Observations on the Ancient Horses of Japan', *JGZ*, LXIV/5, 1956, pp. 197–210.*

HIGUCHI, K., 'Personal Ornaments of the Prehistoric Japanese People', *JRGK*, XIII, 1939, pp. 1–76; XIV, 1940, pp. 77–131.

IMAMURA, Y., AND IKEDA, Z., 'Dr. Kiyono's Theory of the Japanese Race,' *MGK*, XIV/4, 1949, pp. 49–56.*

ISHIDA, E., OKA, M., EGAMI, N., AND YAWATA, I., *Origin of the Japanese People,* Tokyo, 1958.

KAMAKI, Y., 'The Remains of Iijima, Kagawa Prefecture', *SJ*, IV, 1957, pp. 1–11.

KINDAICHI, K., 'The Theory that the Ainu were Ezo', *MGK*, XIII/1, 1948, pp. 1–20.

KIYONO, K., *Currents of Peoples and Cultures in the Pacific*, Tokyo, 1944; *Japanese Racial Theory based on the Study of Ancient Skeletons*, Tokyo, 1949.

KOBAYASHI, Y., *Study of the Ancient Tomb Choshi-zuka, Tanaka, Ikisan Village, Itoshima County, Fukuoka Prefecture*, Kyōto, 1952.*

KOBAYASHI, Y., AND MORIMOTO, R., *Album of Yayoi Pottery*, Ōsaka, 1939.

KODAMA, K. (general editor), *An Illustrated Cultural History of Japan*, I, Tokyo, 1956.

KOMAI, K., 'Stone Circles in Japan', *KGZ*, XXXVIII/1, 1952, pp. 54–64; XXXVIII/5–6, 1952, pp. 22–34.*

KŌNO, H., AND NATORI, T., 'Prehistory of Hokkaidō', *JRGK*, VI, 1938, pp. 1–41.

KŌNO, I., *Jōmon Pottery*, Tokyo, 1953.

KOYAMA, F., TANAKA, S., MITSUOKA, T., AND MIZUNO, S. (editors), *Catalogue of World's Ceramics*, I, Tokyo, 1958.*

MATSUMOTO, N., FUJITA, R., SHIMIZU, J., AND ESAKA, T., *Kamo: a Study of the Neolithic Site and a Neolithic Dugout Canoe Discovered in Kamo, Chiba Prefecture*, Tokyo, 1952.*

MATSUO, T., 'A Preliminary Report on the Investigation on the Dolmens in Hayamajiri', *KGZ*, XXXIX/1, 1953, pp. 45–7*; *A Study of the Stone Tombs in Northern Kyūshū*, Saga City, 1957.

MIKI, F., *Haniwa*, Tokyo, 1958*; *The Beauty of Haniwa*, Tokyo, 1956.

MITSUMORI, S., *The Primitive Culture of Japan*, Tokyo, 1941.

MIYAKE, S., 'Burials in the Japanese Stone Age', *JRGK*, XV, 1940, pp. 1–26.

MIYAKE, Y., AND TAKAHASHI, K., *Haniwa in the Collection of the Tokyo Imperial Museum*, 2 vols., Tokyo, 1919.

MIYASAKA, E., 'The Prehistoric Village Site at Yosukeone on the western slope of the Yatsugatake', *KGZ*, XXXVI/4, 1950, pp. 47–51.*

MIYASAKA, E., AND YAWATA, I., *Togaruishi*, Kayano, 1957.

MIZUNO, S., AND IMANISHI, K., *Life in Primitive Times*, Tokyo, 1950.

MIZUNO, S., HIGUCHI, T., AND OKAZAKI, T., *Tsushima*, Tokyo and Kyōto, 1953.*

MORIMOTO, R., *Studies in Japanese Archaeology*, Kyōto, 1943.

MORINAGA, S. (editor), *Excavated Carbonized Rice*, Tokyo, 1954.

NAKAYA, J., rev. S. UMEHARA, *Handbook on the Stone Age of Japan*, Tokyo and Kyōto, 1943.

ŌBA, I. (general editor), *Hiraide: Synthetic Study on the Remains of Ancient Villages at Sōga Village, Nagano Prefecture*, Tokyo, 1955.*

ŌGA, I., 'On the Cloth Impressions on the Bottom of Yayoi Type Pottery,' *KK*, X, 1955, pp. 4–8.*

OKAZAKI, T., 'Early Iron Implements in Japan, with Special Reference to the finds at Karakami, Harunotsuji, on Iki Island,' *KGZ*, XLII/1, 1956, pp. 14–29.*

ŌYAMA, K., KŌNO, I., IKEGAMI, K., AND SUGIYAMA, S., 'Korekawa Studies,' *SGZ*, II/4, 1930.†

ŌYAMA, K., IKEGAMI, K., AND ŌGYU, T., 'The Excavation of the Kasori Shell-mound at Miyako Village, Chiba Province,' *SGZ*, IX/1, 1937, pp. 1–68.†

ŌYAMA, K., MIYASAKA, M., AND IKEGAMI, K., 'The Chronology of the Jōmon Culture of the Stone Age in the Kantō', *SGZ*, II/6, 1931, pp. 1–84.†

SAITŌ, H., 'The Prehistoric house dog: a Catalogue of the Ōyama Institute for Prehistory', *SGZ*, XII/4–6, 1940, pp. 57–169.†

SAITŌ, T., *Illustrations of Japanese Archaeology*, Tokyo, 1955.

SAKAZUME, N., 'General theories on Japanese Prehistoric Stone Implements,' *JRGK*, XIX, 1941, pp. 1–69; *Shell-mounds*, Tokyo, 1949; 'Shell-mounds in the Kantō and Their Pottery', *NM*, 1952, pp. 58–82.

SERIZAWA, C., *Non-Pottery Culture* (Prehistoric Periods, 1), Tokyo, 1957.

SHIMADA, S., 'Studies on the Prehistoric site at Okamoto, Sugu, in the Province of Chikuzen', *KTDKH*, XI, 1930.*

SHIMADA, S., KIYONO, K., AND UMEHARA, S., 'Excavation of the Shell‚mound of Tsugumo, Oshima Village, Asakuchi County, Bitchu Province', *KTDKH*, v, 1920.*

SHIMIZU, J., AND KURATA, Y., *Yayoi Culture* (Primitive Periods, 1), Tokyo, 1957.

SUENAGA, M., *Ancient Weapons of Japan*, Tokyo, 1943; *Haniwa*, Kyōto, 1947; *Old Tombs from the Air*, Tokyo, 1955.

SUENAGA, M., AND KOBAYASHI, Y., 'Study on the Yayoi Type Remains of Karako, Yamato', *KTDKH*, xvi, 1943.

SUGIHARA, S., *The Stone Age Culture of Iwajuku, Gumma Prefecture*, Tokyo, 1956.*

SUMIDA, S., AND OMAIRI, G., *The Remains of Kyūgo Cave*, Nagoya, 1956.

TAKAHASHI, K., *A Study on the Imitation Stone Implements Discovered in Tombs*, rev. ed., Tokyo, 1925.

TAKEUCHI, S., MINATO, M., KŌNO, H., ŌBA, T., AND SUGIHARA, S., *Tarukishi Excavation Report*, Hakodate, 1956.*

TAKIGUCHI, H. (editor), *Kinrei‚zuka*, Tokyo, 1952.*

TERASHI, M., *Jōmon Pottery in Southern Kyūshū*, Ōguchi, 1954.*

TOKYO IMPERIAL UNIVERSITY, *Album of Specimens in the Institute of Archaeology*, 8 vols., 1927–36.

UMEHARA, S., *Study on the Samida and Shinyama Tombs*, Kyōto, 1921; 'Corpus of Gold Ear‚pendants, Ring‚shaped Pommels of Swords, and Deer Antler Work Ornaments for Swords and Knives in Japan', *KTDKH*, viii, 1923; *A Study of Bronze Bells*, Tokyo, 1927; 'Report of Research on the Stone Age site of Ōgura in the Kitashirakawa District of Kyōto', *Reports of Research on Famous Historical Places in Kyōto Prefecture*, xvi, 1935; 'Corpus of Important Megalithic Stone Chambers of Ancient Tombs in Japan', *KTDKH*, xiv, 1937.

UMEHARA, S., AND KOBAYASHI, Y., 'The Ornamented Tomb Ōtsuka in Kaho County, Chikuzen', *KTDKH*, xv, 1939.*

YAMANOUCHI, S., 'The Main Divisions and Subdivisions of Jōmon Pottery', *SKG*, 1/1, 1937, pp. 29–32; 'A Genealogy of the Custom of Teeth Extraction in Japanese Prehistory', *SKG*, 1/2, 1937, pp. 53–60; *Atlas of Japanese Prehistoric Pottery*, 12 parts, Tokyo, 1940.

YAWATA, I., 'The Stone Age Site at Ubayama: the Shell‚mound and the Ancient Dwellings below the Shell Layer', *Papers of the Anthropological*

Institute of the Imperial University of Tokyo, 5, 1932*; 'The Question of the Religious Beliefs of the Prehistoric Japanese', *JRGK*, XII, 1939, pp. 1–18; XIV, 1940, pp. 19–29; XVIII, 1940, pp. 31–47; *Stone Implements in Japan*, Tokyo, 1948; *The Dawn of Japanese History*, Tokyo, 1953.

YOSHIDA, S., AND ŌTSUKA, H., *The Tomb Culture* (Primitive Periods, II), Tokyo, 1957.

Books and Articles in Western Languages

AKIYAMA, T., 'The Western Cultural Influences in Japan: Prior to the Arrival of Westerners', *Research in Japan in History of Eastern and Western Cultural Contacts*, Japanese National Commission for Unesco, 1957, pp. 133–9.

ASTON, W. G., *Nihongi*, 2 vols., London, 1896.

BATCHELOR, J., *The Ainu of Japan*, London, 1892.

BEARDSLEY, R. K., 'Japan Before History: A Survey of the Archaeological Record', *The Far Eastern Quarterly*, XIV/3, 1955, pp. 317–46.

BUHOT, J., *Histoire des Arts du Japon*, I, Paris, 1949.

CHAMBERLAIN, B. H., *Kojiki*, Tokyo, 1906.

GOWLAND, W., 'The Dolmens and Burial Mounds in Japan', *Archaeologia*, LV, 1897, pp. 439–524.

GROOT, G. J., *The Prehistory of Japan*, New York, 1951.

GROOT, G. J., AND SHINOTŌ, Y., *The Shell Mound of Ubayama*, Ichikawa City, 1952.

HAGUENAUER, C., 'Notions d'archéologie japonaise: le néolithique', *Bulletin de la maison franco-japonaise*, III/1–2, 1931, pp. 1–74; *Origines de la civilisation japonaise*, I, Paris, 1956.

KIDDER, J. E. JR., *The Jōmon Pottery of Japan*, Ascona, 1957. 'The Stone Circles of Ōyu', *Archaeology*, XI/4, 1958, pp. 232–8.

KRAUS, B. S., 'An Outline of Japan's Prehistoric Cultures', *American Antiquity*, XVIII/3, part 2, 1953, pp. 12–16.

MARINGER, J., 'A Core and Flake Industry of Palaeolithic Type from Central Japan', *Artibus Asiae*, XIX/2, 1956, pp. 111–25.

MORI, T., 'Archaeological Study of Jar-Burials in Eneolithic Japan', *Proceedings of the Eighth Pacific Science Congress and the Fourth Far Eastern Prehistory Congress*, Diliman, 1956, pp. 225–46.

MUNRO, N. G., *Prehistoric Japan*, 2nd ed., Yokohama, 1911.

ŌYAMA, K., 'Vorläufiger Bericht über die Chronologie der Jōmon-Kultur der Steinzeit im Kantō (Mittel-Japan)', *Praehistorica Asiae Orientalis*, I, Premier congrès des préhistoriens d'extrême-orient, Hanoi, 1932, pp. 77–90.

PONSONBY-FANE, R. A. B., *Studies in Shintō and Shrines*, rev. ed., Kyōto, 1953.

SCHNELL, I., 'Prehistoric Finds from the Island World of the Far East', *Bulletin of the Museum of Far Eastern Antiquities*, IV, 1932, pp. 15–104.

TORII, R., *Les Ainou des Îles Kouriles*, Tokyo, 1919.

Sources of Illustrations

It has been necessary to redraw several of the text figures in order to provide them with English labels, or for other reasons to supplement them. The following are based on or abstracted from the sources indicated: Maps 1, 4, fig. 62: Kodama, *An Illustrated Cultural History of Japan*, I (figs. 96, 289, 358, 359); Maps 5–7: Suenaga, *Old Tombs from the Air* (figs. 1, 27, 32); fig. 2: Ōyama, 'Kasori Shell-mound' (fig. 14); fig. 3: Mizuno and Imanishi, *Life in Primitive Times* (figs. 96, 114); fig. 28: Matsuo, 'Dolmens in Hayamajiri' (fig. 2); fig. 35: Umehara, 'Megalithic Stone-chambers' (pls. III, IV); fig. 36: Suenaga, *Ancient Weapons of Japan* (figs. 21, 25); figs. 41, 42: Hamada, Umehara and Shimada, 'Ornamented Tombs' (figs. 14, 15); fig. 65: Buhot, *Histoire des Arts du Japon*, I (fig. XVIII). Reproduced by permission of T. Higuchi: fig. 39.

The plates have been provided by the following persons or institutions: National Museum: 6, 9, 12, 16, 18, 22, 49, 53–6, 85, 86, 89, 90, 92, 95, 96, 98–103; Kyōto University: 1–4, 15, 17, 19, 20, 23, 26–9, 36, 37, 40–5, 50, 57–9, 63, 64, 69, 71, 74–7, 79; Metropolitan Museum of Art: 51, 82–4; British Museum: 94; T. Higuchi: 38, 46, 65, 66, 81, 87, 88, 91, 93; Asuka-en: 97; T. Tani: 9; Y. Yamasaki: 22; M. Suenaga: 62; E. Nishihara: 89, 90, 92. Reproduced by permission of M. Suenaga: 60, 61; Y. Kobayashi: 78; S. Yamanouchi: 7, 10; T. Higuchi: frontispiece. Others have been supplied by the author or procured at the site.

3

4

5

6

7

8

9

10

11

12

17

18

19

21

22

23

24

25

26

27

28

29

32

33

38

40

41

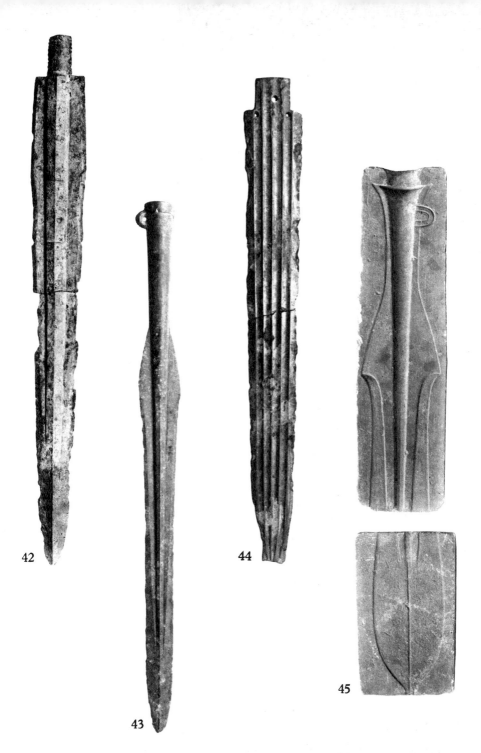

42

43

44

45

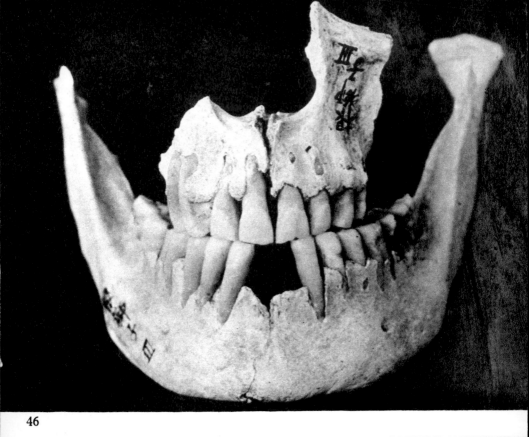

46

47

49

50

51

53

54

55

56

57

58

59

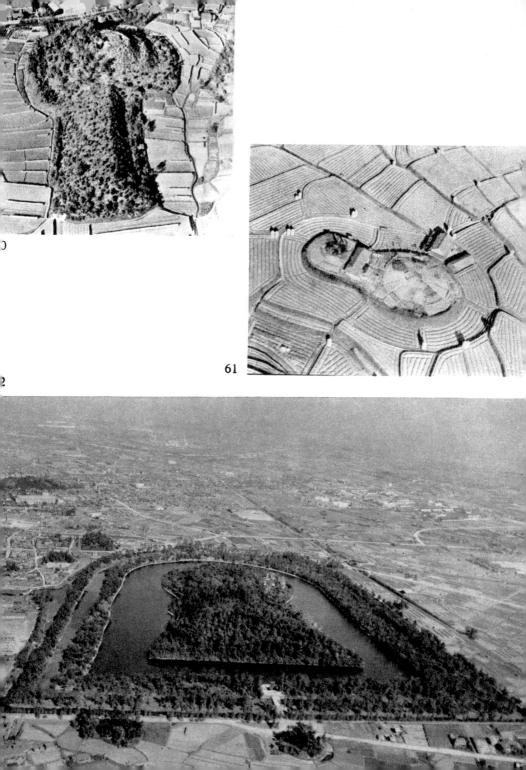

60

61

62

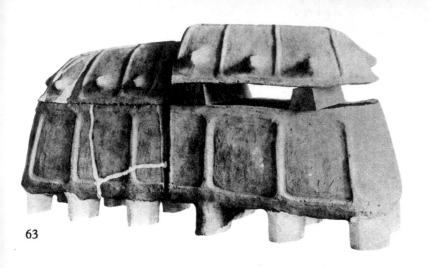

63

64

66

67

68

70

71

76

77

79

80

81

82

83

84

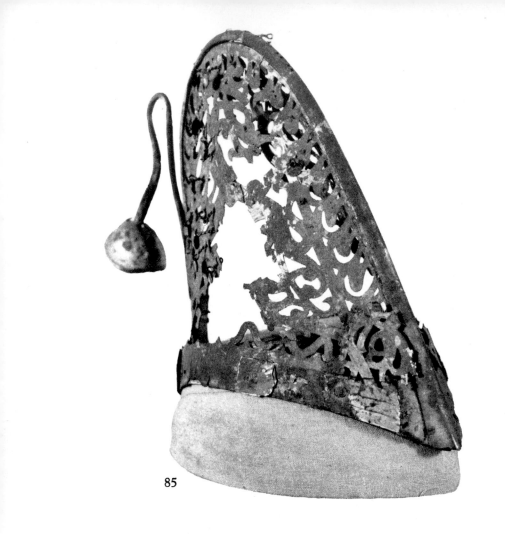

85

86

88

89

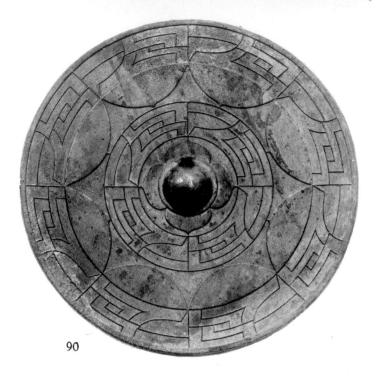

90

91

92

93

94

95

100

101

102

103

106

107

108

Notes on the Plates

Frontispiece: Gilt bronze bridle-bit from Ōtani tomb, Wakayama City. Length 7¼ in. Middle Tomb Period, 5th century A.D. Prefectural Collection.

1 Fireplace of pit-dwelling at Hiromi, Suwa county, Nagano, partially excavated to expose surrounding stones and pottery vessel. Middle Jōmon period.

2 Flexed burial (no. 25) in the Tsugumo shell-mound, Ōshima, Asaguchi county, Okayama, with jar containing infant's bones (no. 26) at head of skeleton. Late Jōmon period.

3, 5 Cryptomeria wood spatulas from Nakai, Korekawa, Sannohe county, Aomori. Length approximately 24 in. Latest Jōmon period.

4 Bone fish-hooks, harpoons and spear points, from Kantō sites. Mostly Late Jōmon period.

6 Pottery vessel from Kamiina county, Nagano. Height $23\frac{7}{8}$ in. Middle Jōmon period. Tokyo National Museum.

7 Pottery vessel from Himi, Himi county, Toyama. Height $15\frac{7}{8}$ in. Middle Jōmon period. Tokyo University.

8 Pottery vessel from Narahara, Nishitama county, Tokyo. Height 10 in. Middle Jōmon period. H. Shiono Collection.

9 Pottery vessel from Horinouchi shell-mound, Ichikawa city, Chiba. Height $16\frac{3}{4}$ in. Late Jōmon period. T. Tani Collection.

10 Pottery vessel from Shiizuka shell-mound, Takata, Inashiki county, Ibaragi. Height $5\frac{1}{4}$ in. Late Jōmon period. Tokyo University.

11 Pottery pouring vessel from Fukuda shell-mound, Ōsuga, Ibaragi. Height 8¾ in. Late Jōmon period. Private Collection.

12 Pottery pouring vessel from Mine-machi, Ōta ward, Tokyo. Height 6⅜ in. Late Jōmon period. Tokyo National Museum.

13 Pottery vessel from Hinokibayashi, Temmabayashi, Kamikita county, Aomori. Height 17⅜ in. Middle Jōmon period. Ōsaka University.

14 Pottery vessel from Enokibayashi, Akagawa, Kamikita county, Aomori. Height 5¼ in. Middle Jōmon period. Ōsaka University.

15 Pottery bowl showing decoration of underside, from Nakai, Korekawa, Sannohe county, Aomori. Latest Jōmon period.

16 Pottery vessel with human figure on the side, from Togoshinai, Susonō, Naka-tsugaru county, Aomori. Height 8½ in. Late Jōmon period. Tokyo National Museum.

17 Clay figurine from Misaka, Higashi-yatsushiro county, Yamanashi. Height 10⅛ in. Middle Jōmon period. Tokyo National Museum.

18 Clay animal from rim of vessel, from Hosaka, Kitakoma county, Yamanashi. Height approximately 4 in. Middle Jōmon period. Tokyo National Museum.

19 Front and back views of clay figurine from Yamamoto, Ikarigaseki, Minami-tsugaru county, Aomori. Latest Jōmon period.

20 Front and back views of clay figurine from Mamuro, Kita-adachi county, Saitama. Height 6¾ in. Latest Jōmon period. T. Nakazawa Collection.

21 Clay figurine from Tokiwasuginodo, Sakuragawa, Isawa county, Iwate, Height 3⁷⁄₁₆ in. Late Jōmon period. Ōsaka University.

22 Clay figurine from Satohara, Iwashima, Agatsuma county, Gumma. Height 11¾ in. Late Jōmon period. Y. Yamasaki Collection.

23 Clay figurine from Kamegaoka, Tateoka, Nishi-tsugaru county, Aomori. Latest Jōmon period.

24 Clay figurine from Kamegaoka, Tateoka, Nishi-tsugaru county, Aomori. Height $2\frac{5}{16}$ in. Latest Jōmon period. Tenri Museum.

25 Back of clay plaque from Kamegaoka, Tateoka, Nishi-tsugaru county, Aomori. Height $3\frac{1}{16}$ in. Latest Jōmon period. Tenri Museum.

26 Clay mask from Aso, Nanakura, Kita-akita county, Akita. Maximum width across $5\frac{5}{8}$ in. Latest Jōmon period. Tokyo National Museum.

27 Curved sandstone object from Tamuko, Taira, Higashi-tonami county, Toyama. Length 9 in. Probably Late Jōmon period. Private Collection.

28 Object carved from deer antler from Miyatojima, Monō county, Miyagi. Latest Jōmon period. Private Collection.

29 So-called 'shoe-shaped' stone implement from Nakagawa, Takaoka city, Toyama. Length about 10 in. Middle-Late Jōmon period. Private Collection.

30 Sun-dial arrangement of stones of the Nonakadō circle, Ōyu, Akita. Height of standing stone 38 in. Late Jōmon period.

31 Stones outlining a rectangle believed to be a grave, Manza circle, Ōyu, Akita. Late Jōmon period.

32 Ainu performing a dance in front of a thatched dwelling. Shiraoi, Hokkaidō.

33 Stone with engraved pictures of salmon at Yajima, Yuri county, Akita. Approximate length of stone 60 in. Late-Latest Jōmon period.

34 Reconstructed dwelling at Toro, Shizuoka city, Shizuoka. Yayoi period type.

35 Aerial view of part of Toro site, Shizuoka city, Shizuoka, showing eleven remains of dwellings, reconstructed house and storehouse. Shizuoka Museum in upper right hand corner. Middle-Late Yayoi period.

36 Clay vessel with suspension basket fragments at Karako excavation, Kawahigashi, Shiki county, Nara. Early-Middle Yayoi period.

37 Well formed of hollowed-out tree trunk at Karako, Kawahigashi, Shiki county, Nara. Early-Middle Yayoi period.

38 Paths between rice paddies lined with wooden battens at Toro, Shizuoka city, Shizuoka. Middle-Late Yayoi period.

39 Cist tomb and jar burial cemetery in process of excavation, near Haruno-tsuji, Iki Island. Three cist tombs and six double-jar burials are visible. Middle Yayoi period.

40 Group of clay vessels found together during the excavation of the Karako site, Kawahigashi, Shiki county, Nara. Early-Middle Yayoi period.

41 Excavation of a double-jar burial in the cemetery at Sugu, Kasuga, Chikushi county, Fukuoka. Burial no. 4 was oriented north-south, placed at a 30° angle, and had a total length of 78 in. Middle Yayoi period.

42 Bronze dagger from Sugu, Kasuga, Chikushi county, Fukuoka. Length about $13\frac{1}{2}$ in. Middle Yayoi period.

43 Bronze spearhead from Mie, Minami-takagi county, Nagasaki. Length $21\frac{7}{16}$ in. Probably Middle Yayoi period. Nagasaki Prefectural Library.

44 Bronze fluted sword found under a large stone in 1899 at Sugu, Kasuga, Chikushi county, Fukuoka. Middle Yayoi period.

45 Parts of sandstone moulds for spearheads, from Sugu, Kasuga, Chikushi county, Fukuoka. These fragments apparently belong to two separate moulds. Taken together the length is $34\frac{1}{2}$ in. Middle Yayoi period. Kumano Shrine.

46 Mandible and maxillary bone from Nijiko, Hirado Island, showing removal of incisor teeth. Yayoi period.

47 Detail of geometric relief on back of circular bronze mirror with two off-centre knobs and semicircular sectioned rim, from Kashiwara-machi, Naka-kawachi county, Ōsaka. Diameter about $8\frac{3}{4}$ in. Probably Middle Yayoi period. Tokyo National Museum.

48 Bronze bell from Fukuda, Fukugi, Asa county, Hiroshima. Height $7\frac{1}{4}$ in. Probably Middle Yayoi period. Private Collection.

49 Bronze bell from Kihi, Kinosaki county, Hyōgo. Middle Yayoi period. Tokyo National Museum.

50 Bronze bell with clapper-ring, from Sumiyoshi, Higashi-nada ward, Kobe. Height $19\frac{1}{4}$ in. Middle or Late Yayoi period. Tokyo National Museum.

51 Bronze bell probably from the Kansai district. Height $43\frac{1}{2}$ in. Late Yayoi period. Metropolitan Museum of Art.

52 Six of twelve panels of relief on a bronze bell traditionally from Kagawa. One side: jumping man holding a stick, two people pounding rice, a raised storehouse; other side: two cranes, a man and dogs hunting a boar, tortoise eating fish. Height of bell $14\frac{3}{4}$ in. Probably Middle Yayoi period. H. Ōhashi Collection.

53 Clay vessel from Fukui, Mishima county, Ōsaka. Late Yayoi period. Tokyo National Museum.

54 Clay vessel from Iwato, Nishi-usuki county, Miyazaki. Height $9\frac{3}{4}$ in. Late Yayoi period. Tokyo National Museum.

55 Clay vessel from Atsuta, Nagoya city, Aichi. Height $12\frac{3}{16}$ in. Late Yayoi period. Tokyo National Museum.

56 Clay vessel with human face, from Osakata, Shimodate, Makabe county, Ibaragi. Height 27 $\frac{3}{16}$ in. Middle Yayoi period. Tokyo National Museum.

57 Clay vessel with combed patterns, from Karako, Kawahigashi, Shiki county, Nara. Height 9$\frac{1}{8}$ in. Middle Yayoi period. Kyōto University.

58 Clay vessel with red painted designs, from Karako, Kawahigashi, Shiki county, Nara. Height 7 $\frac{5}{16}$ in. Early Yayoi period. Kyōto University.

59 Clay vessel with incised design of two men on a boat, from Karako, Kawahigashi, Shiki county, Nara. Height 11 $\frac{3}{16}$ in. Early-Middle Yayoi period. Kyōto University.

60 Chausuyama tomb, Sakurai, Shiki county, Nara. Early Tomb period.

61 Nabeyama tomb, Minami-kawachi county, Ōsaka. Late Tomb period.

62 Tomb of Emperor Nintoku at Mozu, Sakai city, Ōsaka. The largest tomb, with three surrounding moats. Total length about 2695 ft. Middle Tomb period.

63 Clay coffin made in sections, from Nogata, Ōno, Aita county, Okayama. Length 71 in. Late Tomb period.

64 Opened chamber showing hollowed out floor of Hyotanyama tomb, Azuchi, Shiga. Early Tomb period.

65, 66 Excavation of Iwasakiyama tomb, Tsuda, Ōgawa county, Kagawa, showing log-shaped sarcophagus in small chamber before and after removal of lid. Interior head-rests at each end. Early Tomb period.

67, 68 Two views in chamber of the West tomb, Monjuin, Shiki county, Nara, looking toward entrance and back where a Buddhist Fudō has been standing since early historic times. Late Tomb period.

69 Vaulted interior of Marukumayama tomb, Susenji, Itoshima county, Fukuoka. Middle Tomb period.

70, 71 Exterior and interior of tomb known as Ishibutai, Takaichi, Takaichi county, Nara. Late Tomb period.

72 Decorated stone house-shaped sarcophagus in Sekijinyama tomb, Hiro-kawa, Yame county, Fukuoka. Late Tomb period.

73 Concentric circles and other motifs painted on the back wall of the Hinooka tomb, Chitose, Ukiha county, Fukuoka. Late Tomb period.

74, 75 Two views in main chamber of the Ōtsuka tomb, Kaho county, Fukuoka. Late Tomb period.

76 Reliefs carved in rock outside cave at Nabeta, Shikamoto county, Kuma-moto. Late Tomb period.

77 Reliefs carved in rock outside cave called Vault no. 7, at Ō, Ishinuki, Tamana county, Kumamoto. Late Tomb period.

78 Suit of iron armour from Nagamochiyama, Dōmyōji, Minami-kawachi county, Ōsaka. Not shown are the upper and lower leg-guards, and cheek-guards that were attached to the helmet. Middle Tomb period. Kyōto University.

79 Iron helmet with neck guard strips from Kameyama tomb, Arita, Hyōgo. Height including plume holder $7\frac{5}{8}$ in. Middle Tomb period.

80 Bronze arrowheads from Myōkenyama tomb, Sakyo ward, Kyōto city. Length of largest $2\frac{1}{8}$ in. Middle Tomb period. Kyōto University.

81 Bronze bird-headed pommel of sword from uncertain site in Ukiha county, Fukuoka. Width about 3 in. Late Tomb period. Yame High School.

82 Gilt bronze perforated horse flank ornament from Jinda, Mikuri, Tano county, Gumma. Length $5\frac{3}{8}$ in. Late Tomb period. Metropolitan Museum of Art.

83 Bronze jingle-bell ornament for horse flank, from Shintaku, Ōsato county, Saitama. Length 4¾ in. Middle-Late Tomb period. Metropolitan Museum of Art.

84 Bronze horse bells of uncertain provenance. Height of largest 6¾ in. Late Tomb period. Metropolitan Museum of Art.

85 Gilt bronze head-dress from Funayama tomb, Kikusui, Tamana county, Kumamoto. Korean in origin. Height $8\frac{5}{16}$ in. Tomb period. Tokyo National Museum.

86 Gilt bronze shoes from Eta, Tamana county, Kumamoto. Length $13\frac{3}{16}$ in. Late Tomb period. Tokyo National Museum.

87 Bronze jingle-bell mirror from Bentenzuka tomb, Fukuchiyama city, Kyōto. Diameter (excluding bells) $5\frac{7}{16}$ in. Middle-Late Tomb period. Kyōto University.

88 Bronze TLV mirror from Shinyama tomb, Umami, Kita-katsuragi county, Nara. Diameter 9½ in. Middle Tomb period. Tokyo National Museum.

89 Bronze mirror with decoration of four buildings, from Takarazuka tomb, Kawai, Kita-katsuragi county, Nara. Diameter $9\frac{3}{16}$ in. Early Tomb period. Imperial Household Collection.

90 Bronze mirror with geometric patterns, from Shinyama tomb, Umami, Kita-katsuragi county, Nara. Diameter $11\frac{3}{16}$ in. Middle Tomb period. Imperial Household Collection.

91 Bronze mirror with deities and winged animals, from Yamichi Nagatsuka tomb, Ōhaka, Fuwa county, Gifu. Diameter $8\frac{5}{16}$ in. Middle Tomb period.

92 Bronze mirror with hunting scenes, from Yawatanohara, Gumma. Diameter $7\frac{5}{16}$ in. Middle Tomb period. Imperial Household Collection.

93　Five Sue pottery vases attached to a circular support, from Kanegasaki tomb, Nishi-kawatsu, Matsue city, Shimane. Height approximately 4½ in. Late Tomb period. Kyōto University.

94　Sue pottery vase with boat, men and animals on the shoulder; of uncertain provenance. Height 13⅛ in. Late Tomb period. British Museum.

95　Sue pottery libation vase on perforated pedestal with cups, human figures and animals around shoulder, from Kokufu, Oku county, Okayama. Late Tomb period. Tokyo National Museum.

96　Front and back of fully equipped clay *haniwa* warrior, from Kuai, Nitta county, Gumma. Height 53³⁄₁₆ in. Late Tomb period. Tokyo National Museum.

97　Clay *haniwa* lady from Ojima, Nitta county, Gumma. Late Tomb period.

98　Clay *haniwa* lady from Yagi, Isezaki city, Gumma. Height 50½ in. Late Tomb period. Tokyo National Museum.

99　Clay *haniwa* dancers from Ojima, Nitta county, Gumma. Height of larger 13⅜ in. Late Tomb period. Tokyo National Museum.

100　Clay *haniwa* dog with collar and bell, from Sakai, Sawa county, Gumma. Height 18½ in. Late Tomb period. Tokyo National Museum.

101　Clay *haniwa* horse, saddled and with trappings, from Kumagawa city, Saitama. Height 33 in. Late Tomb period. Tokyo National Museum.

102　Clay *haniwa* boat from Saitobaru tomb, Saito, Koyu county, Miyazaki. Length 35 in. Middle Tomb period. Tokyo National Museum.

103　Clay *haniwa* building from Saitobaru tomb, Saito, Koyu county, Miya-zaki. Height 20¹³⁄₁₆ in. Middle Tomb period. Tokyo National Museum.

104　Great Shrine of Izumo, Shimane, seen across the double fence that sur-rounds it and other smaller shrine buildings. Largely rebuilt in 1874.

273

105 One of the four identical buildings at Sumiyoshi Shrine, near Ōsaka city. Reconstructed in 1862.

106 Small building near Outer Shrine, Ise Shrine, Mie. This is a replica of the main shrine and lesser buildings inside the actual shrine precinct. Built in 1953.

107, 108 Two of four male and female figures which stand in front of the tomb of Kibi-hime-no-Miko Hinokuma at Sakaai, Nara. Height of male figure above ground 39$\frac{13}{16}$ in.; female 28$\frac{7}{16}$ in. Probably seventh century A.D.

Index